Then Simon Peter, who was behind him,

arrived and went into the tomb. He saw

the strips of linen lying there, as well as

the burial cloth that had been around Jesus'

head. The cloth was folded up by itself,

separate from the linen.   John 20 : 6 7

The Carpenter's Cloth

IN MEMORY OF
RICHARD LEE VANDERLIND

THE CARPENTER'S CLOTH

Copyright 1997 by Sigmund Brouwer

Published by Word Publishing, a division of Thomas Nelson Inc.,
Nashville, Tennessee 37214

Project Editor—Terri Gibbs

Lyrics from all songs by Cindy Morgan are taken from the album *The Loving Kind*
© 1997 Cindy Morgan and are used by permission.

All Scripture quotations in this book, except those noted otherwise, are from the
New International Version of the Bible (NIV), copyright © 1983 by the International
Bible Society. Used by permission of Zondervan Bible Publishers.

J. Countryman is a trademark of Word Publishing, a division of Thomas Nelson, Inc.

A J. Countryman Book

Designed by Koechel Peterson and Associates, Inc.
Minneapolis, Minnesota

ISBN: 0-8499-5366-9

Printed and bound in Belgium

The Carpenter's Cloth

Sigmund Brouwer

WORD PUBLISHING
Nashville • London • Vancouver • Melbourne

Contents

Preface

I cannot pretend to be a historian. In writing this book I could only do my best as a novelist to reshape and bring to life what I have learned from great writers and historians. I owe them much for enabling me to see these events with new eyes. I especially recommend time with Alfred Edersheim as he shares passionate history and deep faith in his book, *The Life and Times of Jesus the Messiah.*

Because I came to this book as a novelist, I hope readers will indulge my decision to fix a specific place or time or character to some of these essays and vignettes. I wanted to journey alongside the man who accepted death on a cross for all of us. My intent was to remain true to Scripture and to historical facts; I ask forgiveness should my efforts appear to fail in that regard.

I owe special thanks to Jack Countryman and Terri Gibbs for their wonderful vision and equally wonderful patience in shaping this book.

Most of all, I am deeply grateful to my wife, Cindy. During my time with this book, she was in the process of writing the music and lyrics to *The Loving Kind,* an album that explores the same days of Jesus' journey to the cross and beyond. That she and I were able to share time in Galilee as preparation for these endeavors was a joy; that she encouraged me as she did was a gift; that I was able to listen to her songs was joyous inspiration.

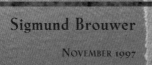

Sigmund Brouwer

NOVEMBER 1997

From boy to a man
  The carpenter's hands
  Healed all the sick and
      diseased,
  Gave hope to the bleak,
  strength to the weak,
  And gave us a song to sing.

CINDY MORGAN
FROM "IN THE GARDEN"

Follow the Carpenter

WHEN JESUS EARNED HIS LIVING AS A CARPENTER, THE craftsman's life then was not much different than now.

Going from job site to job site required travel, for the house does not come to the carpenter. And while a man's reputation depended on the quality of his work, practicality and purpose meant everything, so a carpenter could not afford to spend days perfecting a job that might take others only a few hours to complete. During the construction of a house, a carpenter would have to work in harmony with many types of craftsmen.

It is not hard to see how this background shaped Jesus' ministry.

He did not wait for people to come to him but traveled to reach them.

The spiritual advice Jesus offered his listeners was practical and purposeful and to the point—applicable to everyday life in any culture or century.

Harmony? His twelve disciples ranged in extremity from Andrew and Judas, rebel Zealots sworn to overthrow Roman rule, to Matthew, who collected taxes for those same hated Romans.

All of this is something to take to heart as we consider what we can do to add meaning to our own faith.

Reach out.

Help on a practical level.

Understand and tolerate.

Follow Jesus? Follow the carpenter.

Lazarus

> Jesus loved Martha
> and her sister
> and Lazarus.
>
> JOHN 11:5

To be buried in a tomb instead of a common cemetery indicated a person's social standing in life. Not just the extremely rich, but the middle to upper middle class of that time had their own tombs. Private property purchased long before the need, the burial chambers were hewn by stone workers ahead of time to custom fit the body sizes of the owner and his family members.

BECAUSE OF HIS LOVE OF JESUS, IT IS REMARKABLE THAT Lazarus was allowed a customary Jewish funeral.

Jesus, after all, had become a well-known and dangerous renegade in the eyes of the religious authorities. In the temple on his previous visit to Jerusalem, Jesus had nearly been stoned for blasphemy (John 10:22–39). Later, Jesus announced he was returning to Lazarus in Bethany, a town only two miles from Jerusalem. The disciples feared for his life, so much that Thomas declared he intended to die with Jesus (John 11:16).

Lazarus, of course, was a friend of this renegade, to the point that "Jesus loved Martha and her sister and Lazarus." Yet the synagogue leaders did not seriously consider Lazarus a follower of Jesus. Otherwise they would have declared him apostate, outside of their religion—and the funeral would have been much different.

At the burial of an apostate, for example, the Jews of that time were expected to inflict as many indignities as possible, even to the point of wearing festive white garments to show joy at the death of such a sinner.

The opposite, however, happened after the death of Lazarus. "Many Jews had come to Martha and Mary to comfort them in the loss of their brother" (John 11:19). Nor was this comfort given lightly. We learn later in the narrative that these Jews were still in the house with Mary when Jesus arrived in Bethany, after Lazarus had already been in the tomb four days. Four days! These friends had set aside everything else in their lives to be with Martha and Mary in their time of need.

So, was Lazarus merely a close friend of Jesus but not a believer? Or was he a believer in secret, unwilling to lose his public reputation by openly declaring faith in the man who called himself God's Son?

Either way, Jesus still loved Lazarus. Either way, Jesus did not turn his back on Lazarus but returned to Bethany. Either way, Jesus still sought Lazarus.

Jesus ordered the stone taken away from the entrance of the tomb so that light pierced the inner darkness.

Jesus prayed to the Father on behalf of Lazarus.

Then came that awesome command as Jesus called to a man he loved: *Lazarus, come out!*

A moment of silence penetrated the air outside the tomb. People in the crowd exchanged looks of doubt. Others wondered, with fear, if Jesus truly did have this power. As the moments passed, all eyes were on the tomb entrance.

Lazarus, come out!

In those long, silent moments, what was happening inside the tomb? Most certainly, Lazarus heard the call. But he still had to respond. Jesus did not go into the tomb, he waited for Lazarus to walk out of the tomb— away from death.

In the same way that he sought Lazarus, Jesus seeks and calls each of us—no matter how much our lives and reputations might cast doubts on our relationship with him.

And no matter how much Jesus calls us, he still leaves the choice to us. We can remain in the darkness of death. Or, like Lazarus on that glorious day, we can step into the sunlight, into the embrace of Jesus.

Had Jesus arrived earlier than four days, the raising of Lazarus from death would have seemed less miraculous. Many Jews of that day believed that the soul stayed near the body for three days, waiting in hope to be able to reenter the body. More specifically, the Jews thought that the body did not begin to corrupt until the fourth day. They held that death arrived with a drop of gall from the sword of the angel of death and that as this drop of gall changed the body's face on the fourth day, the soul finally left its resting place near the body. Thus, once the fourth day began, Mary, Martha, and all the mourners would finally have decided that Lazarus was dead beyond all hope.

Mary's Gift

> While he was in
> Bethany, reclining at
> the table of a man
> known as Simon the
> Leper, a woman came
> with an alabaster jar
> of very expensive
> perfume, made of pure
> nard. She broke the
> jar and poured the
> perfume on his head.
>
> MARK 14:3

*T*HE BASIC FACTS ARE SIMPLE AND EASY TO UNDERSTAND. An alabaster jar was a flask made of alabaster stone, itself an object of beauty.

Mary broke it.

Nard, from India, was a rare perfume kept in its pure form, undiluted with less expensive perfumes. The cost of this perfume could have provided enough bread for 5,000 men and their families. It was worth a year's wages.

Mary emptied it over Jesus.

This blatant "waste" not only shocked Judas (who could only think how he might have kept it for himself) but all the other onlookers at the meal, who "rebuked her harshly."

Of the men at that table, only Jesus understood.

Mary loved this great teacher. She had seen him kneel to speak to children. Watched him smile and joke. Been filled with awe at the healings he performed. Seen compassion in his every word and touch.

In a patriarchal society where a woman could suffer divorce if her husband disliked her cooking, Jesus was different from other men. He spoke to women, listened to women, included them in his parables, and even taught them—something not allowed in the synagogues.

How could Mary *not* love this man?

Undoubtedly, she had heard Jesus predict his own death many times. Yet unlike the men around him who pushed those thoughts aside, she took his words to heart. What sorrow it gave her to contemplate his death. This growing sorrow led her to either save or purchase this nard at considerable sacrifice to herself. Mary wanted to be prepared with the best perfume to honor him in death.

And now, at this supper, she was filled with dread. After all the predictions of his own death, she knew Jesus' time was near. The religious authorities had made it clear they wanted to stone him, yet he was determined to go into Jerusalem anyway.

Her sorrow overwhelmed her.

Here was Jesus. Talking. Laughing. Smiling. And all the while she could only think of the terrible moment when he would be lost to her.

Driven by overwhelming sorrow, Mary decided to show Jesus her love while he was still alive, not while she wept over his cold, still body.

She wanted Jesus to know how much she cared—so much that she was willing to make a fool of herself in front of the men who surrounded him.

Imagine how it would devastate and humiliate her to be rejected—not privately, but publicly. In front of men who could not understand what emotion drove her to this act.

Yet Jesus, her wonderful friend, did not let her down. He saw past the undeniable logic of caring for the poor. He saw the earnestness of her love. He saw her sorrow. And most of all, he saw her vulnerability.

Jesus did not reject her.

He was touched by her love. He rebuked the others, and made a promise that Mary would be remembered wherever the gospel was preached in the world.

Such is the One she loved.

The Donkey Colt

"Go to the village ahead of you, and as you enter it, you will find a colt tied there, which no one has ever ridden. Untie it and bring it here."

Luke 19:30

TWO MEN APPROACH BETHPAGE ON FOOT. PETER, THE red-headed one on the right with a sword strapped to his side, wears the rough clothing of a fisherman—and a perpetual scowl of suspicion common to laborers who understand no way to make money except with their hands. The other, John, is taller, with thinning brown hair. He walks with a staff. As they near Bethpage, unlike the pilgrims, they peer ahead not for their first view of Jerusalem, but for a donkey colt.

As they enter the hamlet, John points ahead. A colt is tethered to a post outside the doorway of an inn.

"Remarkable, is it not?" John asks, shaking his head in admiration. "It is right where he said it would be."

"Hardly worth talking about," Peter snorts. "Remember Lazarus?"

They approach the colt. A group of men are gathered nearby, older men on chairs in front and younger men standing behind, amusing themselves with comments about passersby.

"I don't like this," Peter says. "It would have been better if he had sent Judas with some money. Why should they let us just take the colt?"

"Walk proud," John answers. "Keep your faith. You know who sends us."

At the inn, Peter and John smile and nod with the awkwardness of latecomers to a party. Peter, remembering his faith, bends his head and begins to untie the colt.

"You!" a man nearby challenges, stepping toward them. "What are you doing?"

Peter says nothing, knowing that Jesus is a man of peace.

"You!" the man repeats. "Are you deaf? Touched in the head?"

Peter straightens, his hands on the halter rope. He can stay patient only so long. "I hear you with no difficulty. As for my head, it is perfectly—"

"Ho, ho," the man laughs with the assurance of one accustomed to brawls. "But a few words and I can tell you're from the north. All they grow up there are simpletons."

He pauses, looking to his companions for support; their grins are more than enough encouragement for him. "So tell me, country boy, what are you doing?"

The tendons on the side of Peter's neck strain as he tries to control his temper.

"This is a rope," Peter explains. "The rope is attached to the colt. My fingers are upon the rope. As my fingers pull apart the knot, the rope becomes untied. Once I untie the rope, the colt will be free. It is a simple concept. Surely even the dimmest of minds can . . ."

"Peace, Peter," John interrupts. "Think peace. And remember our instructions."

"Bad enough *they* cut me short," Peter hisses. "But you. If I don't get a chance to speak a full sen—"

John speaks directly to the men, remembering the Master's instructions. "Our Lord needs this colt. He will send it back shortly."

The men nearby protest. Why would two complete strangers take a colt that doesn't belong to them? An older man in front, his beard totally gray, calls for silence.

"Tell me," the older man says, speaking to John. "This Lord of yours. Would he happen to be the Prophet from Nazareth?"

"None other," John replies.

"We have heard rumors of his arrival," the old man says. "Will he pass by here?"

John nods.

The old man thinks for several seconds. "The story about a dead man. Lazarus of Bethany. Were you there? Is it true?"

"Words cannot do it justice," Peter claims stoutly. "I smelled the stench of death myself. And out of the darkness Lazarus came forth, called by our Lord."

The others begin to whisper among themselves.

The old man makes his decision. There can be no harm and possibly great gain in extending a favor to a famous worker of miracles. "Take the colt, then."

As Peter unties the halter, John smiles at the old man.

"Tell me," John asks the man, "has this colt been ridden before?"

"It is unused," the man replies. "Why?"

"No reason," John says. "Idle curiosity."

Peter glances over the colt's head at John. They smile at each other. The Master was wise enough to foresee why they would be allowed to take the colt; divine enough to know it had never been ridden.

Their private moment passes, and they lead the colt back toward Bethany where Jesus has already begun to lead a procession on foot.

As soon as Peter and John turn a corner in the road, the young men in front of the inn scatter to spread the news in all directions, taking ownership in the arrival of the miracle man of Nazareth by proudly being the first to spread the word.

As for the older men, they merely wait by the side of the road. They have long since learned that most of life's important events seem to arrive with or without their efforts. Nor do they intend to lose their vantage point.

The arrival of the man of Galilee promises to be an event worth remembering, one never again to be repeated in history— divinity passing by on a colt.

Palm Sunday

As he approached
Jerusalem and saw the
city, he wept over it. . . .

LUKE 19:41

A GIRL AND A BOY—SCRUFFY, DIRTY, LOWER CLASS CHILDREN whose parents had little concern for their whereabouts— dodged and twisted through the throng at one side of the road. The boy shot through a gap in front of a man on a donkey and stopped so quickly the girl almost fell on top of him. She lifted her hand to cuff him in playful vexation, but the sight that had mesmerized him stayed her hand. She, too, stared upward in awe.

It was the man on the donkey, riding beneath palm branches held over him like a royal arch. His smile, which had first riveted the boy, was now cast upon the girl. He focused his entire attention upon them both with a gaze of such presence that a silence of instinctive untroubled yearning covered them. So powerful was his smile that years later in occasional quiet moments the memory of it would soothe their souls with a caress as certain as a physical touch.

Followers behind the colt surged forward, and the moment passed as the crowd swept in front of the boy and girl, blocking their view of the man on the colt. Without exchanging words or glances, each turned to follow, trying to squeeze around the legs of the chanting adults. They stayed with the crowd as the road turned slightly downward, dipping out of sight of the corner of

Jerusalem. The road rose again shortly, bringing the Holy City into full view for the first time.

What the children could not see, the man on the colt did.

Here, from the east, it seemed the city rose from a deep abyss—the valleys of Kedron and Hinnom. The temple tower dominated the skyline, the vast temple courts spreading beneath. The monstrous temple walls on the eastern edge of the plateau seemed like cliffs—unassailable and as fixed as eternity. The upper palaces, brilliant white in the sunshine, now threw shadows across the garden terraces and the city below, giving an impression of unearthly splendor and an ache of beauty that could never fully be captured by memory or description.

What the children could not see, the man on the donkey did, as if in that single moment time's curtain rippled just enough to give him a ghastly vision . . .

of earth heaped into ramps reaching the city walls,

of legions of soldiers swarming triumphant,

of a city outline marred by the smoke of destruction,

of proud temple walls shattered into piles of rubble,

of hundreds of rebels dying on crosses too numerous to comprehend,

of wailing mothers searching the ruins for bodies of torn children—and then with another ripple of time, a new vision . . .

of dust swirling in an eerie dance to a dirge sung by the moaning wind as it blew across the desolation of centuries—the rejection by God himself in horrible, cold punishment for a city about to butcher his son.

What the children could not see, the man on the donkey did—the beauty of the city and the inexorable tragedy ahead. The force of the contrast tore loose from him a wrenching sob so loud it startled those beside him. His sorrow deepened into heaving lamentation, spreading a pall of uneasy silence over his followers.

It was as if he spoke to the city when the

agonized words left his mouth. "If only you had known on this day what would bring you peace—but now it is hidden from your eyes. The days will come upon you when your enemies will build an embankment against you and encircle you and hem you in on every side."

He closed his eyes, but could not shut out the vision overwhelming him. "They will dash you to the ground, you and the children within your walls. They will not leave one stone on another, because you did not recognize the time of God's coming to you."

His weeping did not stop.

The boy and the girl crept forward. Unlike the adults, the terrible sorrow of the man on the donkey did not frighten them. It filled them with a longing to comfort him, as though he were a child in need of them. His sorrow drew them slowly to the colt where each shyly rested a hand on the hide of its flank.

For as long as he wept they walked wordlessly and shared his grief.

The March

It was a march of a revolution,
It was a march of a stormy day,
It was a cadence of cruel contention,
It was a march, oh what a march.

Oh it was a march for the sweet
    and gruesome
To bring a light to their darkened
    place,
It was a march for the thirst of
    freedom,
And it was beauty battered and
    bleeding,
And it was a march.

When it all comes down to
    me and you,
Will we walk away or march on with
The one who made the march, oh
    yeah?

Do you know
Why you are lonely?
Do you know
Why you're afraid?

Do you know
That Jesus loves you?
Will you join the march?
Will you join the march
Today?

Oh it was a march for the ones
    who judged him,
Dipping their crowns in a crimson
    flood.
It was a march for the thief and
    harlot,
Humble and Holy, oh what a story,
Oh what a march.

But when it all comes down to me
    and you,
Will we walk away or march on with
The one who made the march?

❀ CINDY MORGAN

The Children's Hosannas

> The blind and the lame came to him at the temple, and he healed them. But when the chief priests and the teachers of the law saw the wonderful things he did and the children shouting in the temple area, "Hosanna to the Son of David," they were indignant.
>
> Matthew 21:14, 15

THINK OF THE CHILDREN.

In the temple with their parents, there are babies in mothers' arms. Young boys, wriggling with energy, are bored by the seriousness they cannot understand. Girls, eyes wide with wonder, faces half hidden by wraps of cloth, sense already that much of the temple will always be barred to them simply because they are not male.

Then comes this man. A man of rage and action. A man who chases animals out of the market. A man who shouts. A man unstopped.

How could the children not be fascinated?

They see the reactions of their parents. Many parents applaud and cheer the man. Gone are the corrupt and hated thieves who exhort money, who inspect animals and sell sacrifices at outrageous prices.

Some parents exchange stories. This is the prophet who raised Lazarus from the dead. Yes, the Pharisees have posted notices that he must be stoned. But listen, the Pharisees cannot stop him because of the crowds that follow.

Other parents, newly arrived in Jerusalem, are astonished, openly asking questions. Who is this man? Why haven't the temple police stopped him? Where is the man going now?

This man is followed, of course. By parents who cheer him, by parents who talk about him, by parents who speculate about him.

The children remain with their parents. So the children, too, are there in the courtyard. They see the miracles that take place on the steps of the temple.

This man touches a crippled beggar—and the beggar dances and sings.

This man speaks to a blind woman—and she weeps with joy, turning her eyes to family members she can finally see.

This man takes away groans and pain—he leaves behind peace.

The children look at the faces of their parents and see entranced wonder. The children look at the face of the man and see God-like love.

Around the children, some who were healed shout hosannas, echoing the welcome this man received as he rode a donkey colt into Jerusalem.

The children are touched by all this joy. They are simpler in heart and mind than their parents, closer to God in their innocence than the adults around them. They cannot help what their souls are called to do.

They burst into loud hosannas. Their sweet voices ring off the temple walls like a melody of angels gathered in a bouquet of praise.

Their hosannas interrupt the temple services, bringing forth stodgy old men with white beards resting on their chests. The old men shout with anger, demanding quiet.

This man in front of them sees through the hypocritical claims of these old men who declare that God must have reverence in his holy house, who demand that the children be silenced. This man admonishes the stern, outraged old men . . . and, to the children's amazement, the old men leave.

The children know. This man has great power.

The children continue to sing hosanna, for truth and love cannot be silenced.

This man Jesus smiles. It is reward enough.

The Barren Fig Tree

> In the morning, as they went along, they saw the fig tree withered from the roots. Peter remembered and said to Jesus, "Rabbi, look! The fig tree you have cursed has withered!"
>
> Mark 11:20–21

ETURNING TO JERUSALEM FROM THE MOUNT OF OLIVES, Jesus and his followers noticed a fig tree in the distance— probably because its green leaves were so obvious in the early growing season. Jesus, hungry and faint from a night of prayer, needed sustenance.

Seeing the green tree against the brown hills, he had good reason to expect to find figs on its branches. It was a common saying in Galilee that the fruit of the fig appeared before the leaves. Yet the tree yielded nothing for Jesus, and he called judgment upon it.

Matthew, who often compressed his narratives, describes the tree's withering as an immediate event; Mark places it the next morning. Matthew has the disciples asking how Jesus did this miracle; Mark gives the question more implicitly, describing how Peter pointed out the withered tree in amazement.

Either way, the tree died in a miraculous way. Either way, Jesus gave an explanation passed on to us by both Gospels.

"Have faith in God," Jesus began, perhaps hoping they would understand immediately that without faith, Israel in its appearance of glory, was as barren of God as the tree had been of figs.

We can understand that the disciples, frail in their humanity, might have been too much in awe of the miracle to comprehend its meaning. A storm calmed, the lame healed, a man raised

from the dead. All of these events, like the withered fig tree, were so incredible it was difficult to look beyond the miracle for meaning.

So Jesus explained further, using a common Rabbinical expression for doing the impossible—"rooting up mountains."

"I tell you the truth," Jesus continued. "If anyone says to this mountain, 'Go, throw yourself into the sea,' and does not doubt in his heart but believes that what he says will happen, it will be done for them."

Perhaps Jesus stopped speaking again, hoping his point would be obvious: Faith, far more than giving power to prayer, is also its foundation.

Faith allows a soul to trust in God and, with this trust, allows prayer to be offered untainted by self-awareness, selfish ambition, or the hard heart of unforgiveness.

In true prayer, the possibilities of faith are without limit.

If the disciples still did not comprehend fully, and if Jesus felt frustration, we can easily hear him continuing with compassion for these devout, unlearned men whom he loved as brothers.

"I tell you then," Jesus said, completing his lesson, "whatever you ask for in prayer, believe that you have received it, and it will be yours. And when you stand praying, if you hold anything against anyone, forgive him, so that your Father in heaven may forgive you."

His teaching complete, it is easy to imagine Jesus looking from one disciple to another. It is also easy to imagine that when his eyes met those of Judas, that disciple flinched and looked away.

With betrayal already in his heart, Judas understood too well the implications of Jesus' judgment against a tree that had denied his desire—whatever resists Jesus will be swept away as surely as the fig tree withered.

Jesus Teaches Parables

To THE UNEDUCATED PEASANTS OF JESUS' TIME, HE WAS AN incredible teacher. These unsophisticated people of poverty lived their entire lives within a few miles of the villages where they were born. They were suspicious of the wealthy, who far too often took advantage of them. They suffered through legalistic admonishments from the self-righteous synagogue authorities.

Jesus did not speak to them from the loftiness of superiority, as a person who knew much more and had seen much more than they. He reached them at their level, illustrating his teaching with stories about the simple, common things in life.

Parables.

Jesus' teaching was effective because he used their language. More importantly, it was effective because he taught abstract concepts by using concrete examples. Jesus, the ultimate communicator, never told his audience what he could show them instead.

He did not tell them to be prepared, he showed them ten bridesmaids waiting for the groom—five foolish and five wise. He did not tell them they were rejecting God's son, he showed them the tenants who killed the vineyard owner's son. He did not tell them to love their neighbors, he showed them the good Samaritan.

The One who is the ultimate in abstractions—truth, righteousness, honor, faithfulness, commitment, and especially love—knows we are beings who rely on sight, sound, touch, taste, and smell to learn about our world.

How then does God teach us to understand these abstractions about himself?

In the way that Jesus taught through parables. Not by telling . . . but by showing.

He sent his Son to live among us.
He gave his Son to die for us.

Temple Thieves

Then he entered
the temple area
and began driving
out those who were
selling. "It is written,"
he said to them,
"My house will be
a house of prayer;
but you have made it
a den of robbers."

Luke 19:45–46

Oren, son of Judd, stands not much taller than the heads of the goats in the enclosure behind him. His robes are woven of finest cloth, and his fingers are heavy with thick rings of gold. What does it matter than the stench of manure clings to his shoes, or that he is dusty with the dirt of livestock? He is a man of power.

Oren has earned his wealth over the years in the same way he is earning it now, examining sacrificial animals. He prides himself on his ability to remain focused even when the pace of commerce is at its most hectic during the yearly madness of Passover.

Around him, filling the Court of the Gentiles, thousands of pilgrims stream past the animal enclosures and money tables, creating a babble of noise broken by shouting merchants and crying children. Cramped against each other in makeshift pens, lambs and goats and oxen mill in nervous circles, the smell of fresh dung scattered by their hooves.

Dozens of pilgrims wait sullenly for Oren to inspect their offerings—small lambs tucked under arms, goats led by ropes, doves in reed cages. In front of him now is an old woman with a lamb.

He turns the lamb upside down and frowns professionally at spots on its belly.

"Unpure," he announces to the elderly woman. "Not fit for sacrifice."

"What's that?" She cups her ears with her hands, trying to hear above the din.

"I cannot give my approval to an animal blemished with spots," he says. She is too dim-sighted to realize the spots are merely dirt. He can clean the lamb later and sell it for great profit. "Without my approval, the priests will not accept it at the altar."

"I brought my healthiest lamb" she protests. "It cannot be."

"Ignorance like yours is why the priests engage a *mumcheh* like me."

"But I am giving God the best that I have!" She is close to weeping.

He shrugs. "Have you spent a year and a half with a farmer learning what faults are temporary and what faults are permanent?"

"No, but—"

"I have. The priest will take my word over yours." He holds out his hands. "I have been authorized to charge six *isar* for my judgment."

Oren clucks self-righteously. "You could have avoided all this trouble by buying your animal at the market here."

"From thieves who ask for a pigeon the cost of a month's food?"

Again, he shrugs. "Do you wish the inconvenience of carrying this impure lamb, or do you wish to leave it with me to dispose of?"

At this final outrage, the woman loses her patience. "I have traveled three weeks to get here. I have paid two denar to change my coins into shekels for the temple tribute. And now you propose to steal the very lamb you have rejected?"

Oren's thick ruddy lips form a waxen smile. "You are welcome to have another mumcheh examine your lamb. For another six isar, of course."

The woman screeches in anger. "You are all thieves! Working together to squeeze blood from our bones! If I were a man I would—"

Voices behind her rise in agreement, until shouts distract all of them.

The prophet

"The prophet! He arrives! It is Jesus, from Nazareth!"

Oren hopes they are wrong . . . but he hears a roar of approval.

Although a dreadful suspicion tells him what to expect, he needs to know for himself. He remembers what happened when Jesus visited before. That time, Oren had been one of the prophet's first victims. He has no intention of seeing his money scattered again.

Groaning with effort, he hauls his fat body up onto a table. It sags under his weight. He totters as he stands and looks over the crowd. What he sees confirms his dread. The lunatic from Nazareth is on another rampage.

Already, Jesus has overturned two money tables. Shekels and pagan coins are scattering like grain; money changers on hands and knees are trying to scoop them together.

Jesus spins the other way, toward the gates of the animal enclosures. He pulls open the gates of a goat pen first and wades in, waving his arms to drive the goats into the crowd. Then the cattle. The sheep and lambs. Finally the oxen.

Above all the confusion, pilgrims cheer, venting their hatred for the temple market.

Oren tumbles from his table as an ox slams against it. He scrambles to avoid the heavy hooves. When he finds his feet, he waddles away to search for a high priest— temple revenue is too important. This Jesus must be stopped before the pilgrims rebel completely.

Yes, Oren assures himself in a steam of rage. Now the high priests will be pressured by all of the temple sellers. Somehow— and permanently—this lunatic from Nazareth must be stopped!

arrives!

By Whose Authority?

> They arrived again in
> Jerusalem, and while
> Jesus was walking in
> the temple courts,
> the chief priests, the
> teachers of the law and
> the elders came to him.
> "By what authority are
> you doing these things?"
> they asked. "And who
> gave you authority
> to do this?"
>
> Mark 11:27–28

EARLY TUESDAY MORNING, A LARGE DELEGATION—PRIESTS, elders, and Caiaphas in the full attire of High Priest— approaches Jesus where he and his twelve disciples are walking in the far corner of an outer temple court.

The delegates have chosen the early hour with purpose; few pilgrims are gathered around to hear Jesus.

When Caiaphas stops, the entire delegation halts with him. The showdown begins—dozens of Jerusalem's most powerful men face a handful of peasants.

Caiaphas, tall and lean as a savage dog, stares across a distance of twenty paces at the prophet from Nazareth. To any other Jew in the land, such a hostile glare from the highest religious authority would have been like a roar from God Himself.

"Let me be clear in front of all these witnesses," Caiaphas states. "I am not suggesting you are a mere Haggadist, a teller of legends and stories. No, I am declaring that you actually teach. Do you deny this?"

Jesus lets a half smile touch his face. He understands. It is a question of great importance.

Teaching was traditional, handed down from teacher to disciple, who in turn, once granted authority, passed on the same teaching, *unchanged*. The most respected scholars were those who recited every teaching, word for word—nothing lost, nothing added. In any discussion, the ultimate appeal was always to an authority, whether to a famous teacher or to the Great Sanhedrin. Anyone who disagreed with the set authorities was either an ignorant scholar or a rebel who faced banning. Unauthorized teaching was simply not permitted.

Jesus nods. Yes, the nod says, he has been teaching in the temple.

Caiaphas triumphantly springs his questions. "By whose authority are you doing these things? And who gave you the authority to do this?"

The questions are phrased to perfection. Now it will not appear that the leaders are challenging this popular man; instead, they are merely protecting the people by verifying his background. After all, if Jesus has done everything attributed to him, the elders must confirm that these acts are not of Beelzebub, the Devil who opposes God.

By whose authority are you doing these things?

And who gave you the authority to do this?

Caiaphas licks his lower lip, anticipating one of three answers. While unlikely, if Jesus actually says Beelzebub, the priests have every right to take him to the temple wall and hurl him into the valley below.

If he quotes a great Jewish teacher as his authority—the revered Hillel, for example—then the people will lose faith in him, for the true Messiah would not be lesser than another man.

The possibility of the third answer, claiming authority from God, gives Caiaphas an anticipation so strong the muscles on his belly tremble. If they hear this answer, they will stone him as a heretic before any crowds can form to protest and protect him.

By whose authority are you doing these things?

And who gave you the authority to do this?

Jesus stares back. He knows the High Priest's mind. Silence makes tension.

"I will ask you one question," Jesus finally replies. He begins so casually, listeners might

guess this is simply another matter of teaching to be discussed. "Answer me, and I will tell you by what authority I am doing these things. John's baptism—was it from heaven? Or from men?"

Abruptly, Jesus raises his voice.

"Tell me!" he commands. His face, gentle and amused, has stiffened to match the sudden anger in his voice. It is as if an invisible mantle of power has been placed upon him, as if Jesus is now judge and the delegation on trial.

Caiaphas actually takes a half step back. And hates the peasant for it.

"We cannot say from man," an elder whispers to Caiaphas with sudden panic. "Once this gets to the people . . ."

Caiaphas does not need the sentence completed. The crowds believed John the Baptist was a prophet sent directly from God. If they answer that John the Baptist's power was from man, the people might riot.

"Nor can we say from heaven . . ." the elder continues, ". . . for then he will ask why we don't believe him and his teachings."

"I have duties at the altar," Caiaphas says in a low voice to the elder. "Debate this among yourselves to keep him waiting. Then tell him we don't know the answer to his question."

Caiaphas makes his face a mask of peaceful contemplation. But thoughts of murder—savage murder with his own hands—heat his mind.

Caiaphas cannot fool himself, let alone anyone who has observed the last few minutes. Word will reach all ears. The mountain had come to the prophet. The great ruling authority of hundreds of generations of religious tradition had challenged a solitary, uneducated peasant carpenter—and lost.

Walking away is retreat. For Caiaphas, the battle has now become personal.

As he leaves the courtyard, he vows silently to use all his wealth, power, and cunning to end the peasant's life.

Hard Heart

(Jesus addresses the Pharisees)

In a shell of bitterness
Covered in self-righteousness,
In the wake of evidence
You're clinging to your stubbornness.
Drinking from a dirty cup,
Well you turn your head
And drink it up,
But the nasty deeds you hide away
Will all be seen on judgment day.

No letting go
Of the old traditions,
Paving the road
With a strong conviction
And the blood flows
For a true redemption.
But you cannot see that you've
gone too far
Cause you live your life
With a hard heart.

Were you looking for an angry king
To help you conquer everything?
But the day will come

When you'll drop your sword and cry:
Blessed be the one who comes
In the name of the Lord.
Snake in the grass, crack in the glass,
You beat down the head
Of the poor and hungry.
Whatever you do to the least of these
You do it unto me, unto me.

No letting go,
And the blood flows
For a true redemption,
But you cannot hear
What the Savior said
Cause your heart is hard,
And your faith is dead,
And you cannot see
That you've gone too far—
Cause you live your life with a
Hard heart.

✿ CINDY MORGAN

What Jesus Stood For

IN JESUS' TIME, THE PHARISEES HAD CLEARLY DEFINED WHAT they stood *against*. Over generations, using the basic laws of the Ten Commandments and the teachings of Moses, they had developed a vast legalistic structure—to the point that they argued whether it was lawful to eat an egg laid on the Sabbath.

They were against travel on the Sabbath. They were against impurity. They were against women in the inner court of the temple. Most of all, in their self-righteousness, they were against the people who failed to follow their religious rules.

Jesus? In the two great commandments—love God, love your neighbor—he stated not what he stood against, but what he stood *for*. For healing, even on a Sabbath. For forgiveness, not of sin but of the sinner. For reaching out to those in need. For love.

And when he died on the cross, Jesus stood for us all.

Public Contest

EARLY IN THE FINAL WEEK, WHEN JESUS SPOKE IN THE TEMPLE, it seemed like a one-sided contest.

The large temple courts, some of them capable of holding tens of thousands of worshipers, literally formed an arena, with spectators crowding the steps around the colonnades where Jesus spoke.

The people saw on one side, lawyers and scribes. White-bearded, white-clothed Pharisees, armed with scrolls. Sadducees dressed with the accouterments of wealth that come with success in politics. Herodians, politically motivated to replace the Roman governor's rule with Herod. Fresh-faced students in black robes, eager for the chance to show their verbal finesse.

In short, Jerusalem's intellectual elite had gathered in full force for a very public display of their considerable debating skills and substantial, collective knowledge of Scripture. To them, here was an upstart who needed a quick lesson in humiliation.

The upstart, of course, was Jesus, facing all of them, alone, a mere carpenter from Nazareth. If his unassuming clothing was not indication enough of his lack of status, every word he spoke in his rough Galilean was a reminder to the audience of his lack of education.

With no television, radio, novels, or movies, this contest was wonderful entertainment, especially for the common people who shared a suspicion of lawyers and the wealthy elite. Especially because Jesus seemed to be winning.

Listen to some of the thrust and parry:

This from Jesus, ". . . have you never read in the Scriptures? 'The stone the builder rejected has become the cornerstone; the Lord has done this, and it is marvelous in our eyes.'"

"Yes, yes," one of the students calls in reply, determined to show off his memorization, "from the book of Psalms. By excellent use of a pun, the author implies that the cornerstone is also a leader. As part of a victory celebration, the author undoubtedly meant to exhort the people to song."

An older man, a Pharisee, speaks with impatience. "It is only a fragment of Scripture. What does this have to do with a tale about the tenants of a vineyard who kill the landowner's son when he arrives to collect the grapes?"

"The kingdom of God will be taken away from you," Jesus replies. "It will be given to a people who will produce its fruit."

"No!" an elderly man shouts, his voice surprisingly powerful. "No! You cannot speak to us like that!"

Jesus only needs to raise an eyebrow in reply. It brings laughter from the crowd, for few of the poorer pilgrims miss

the implications of the man's anger. If these Pharisees and the rest of the elite feel the parable of the vineyard is directed at them, it is their guilty consciences that are pricked to such immediate anger.

The crowd's laughter only increases the anger of the elite. The ignorant peasant from Galilee is besting them.

So the Herodians, members of a political group, along with some Pharisees, their customary enemies, spring the trap. They pose the famous question that Jesus cannot answer without condemning himself.

"Is it right then to pay taxes to Caesar?"

No true Messiah can acknowledge an earthly power; answering "yes" would destroy his power among the people. Yet if he answers "no" to keep his popularity with the masses, the temple police will immediately take him away and charge him with sedition, for the Roman authorities only tolerate local religions to a certain extent. Nor can Jesus decline to answer, for that would be admitting defeat.

The silence lengthens. Until Jesus points to the portrait on a Roman coin, and defeats them with the answer that will live as long as history.

"Give to Caesar what is Caesar's" he says, "and give to God what is God's."

Yes. It was a one-sided contest. In favor of the carpenter.

If the losers want to silence this man, they will have to kill him.

❧

The Poor Widow

Jesus sat down opposite the place where the offerings were put and watched the crowd putting their money into the temple treasury. Many rich people threw in large amounts. But a poor widow came and put in two very small copper coins, worth only a fraction of a penny.

Calling his disciples to him, Jesus said, "I tell you the truth, this poor widow has put more into the treasury than all the others. They all gave out of their wealth; but she, out of her poverty, put in everything—all she had to live on."

Mark 12:41–43

WHEN JESUS OBSERVED THE POOR WIDOW, IT WAS PROBABLY from a series of steps in front of the court of the women. Under the pillared roof surrounding this open court—a space large enough for more than 15,000 worshipers—trumpet-shaped boxes were available for religious and charitable donations. Each box had an inscription to mark the type of contribution: gifts for children of the pious poor, payment for sacrifices, incense for the temple, and so on.

Out of all the people going past these boxes, Jesus noticed the lone figure of a pauper widow.

Perhaps she was an easy figure to notice because of her slow, infirm movements. Perhaps she was an easy figure to notice because she was too embarrassed to mingle with wealthier worshipers. Either way, Jesus watched her closely and saw her drop two small copper coins into the box as her gift to God.

This amount was the least a worshiper could lawfully contribute. Their combined value was the ninety-sixth part of a denarius. As a poor person, the widow undoubtedly had no savings. If she worked as a housekeeper, her gift was the major portion of what she earned in a day.

Yet despite her great sacrifice, Jesus did not direct his encouraging words to her but to the disciples. He allowed the poor widow to shuffle past without blessing her,

without telling her that God in person
   had seen her action,
without promising her a reward,
without thanking her.

We can only imagine how much his words
might have helped her, a woman who faced the
continual struggle of frugal, lonely days until
death claimed her fragile body.

Even as she passed within distance of his
voice, Jesus said nothing to relieve her of this
desolation. In his wisdom he knew what is
easily forgotten by those who give for reasons
other than simple faith: Faith marked by self-
surrender—for her act was surely that—makes
any burden light. With her focus on God
instead of her own concerns, this pauper
widow had no need for an immediate reward.

Why did Jesus remain silent to her?

Perhaps because he knew it would only be
a short silence.

Heaven was waiting for them both.

Whose Son Is the Christ?

While the Pharisees were gathered together, Jesus asked them, "What do you think about the Christ? Whose son is he?"

"The son of David," they replied.

He said to them, "How is it then that David, speaking by the Spirit, calls him 'Lord'? For he says, 'The Lord said to my Lord: "Sit at my right hand until I put your enemies under your feet."'

COULD JESUS BE PLAYFUL?

In the temple, he is surrounded by a mixed crowd: poor people searching for hope; skeptics hoping to see proof of miraculous powers; followers hanging on to every word; Pharisees challenging his teachings.

There is banter. There are occasional catcalls.

When Jesus speaks seriously, the crowd is silent. When Jesus pauses and rests, or engages in quiet conversation with a few people close to him, others in the crowd discuss the happenings with each other.

Perhaps there comes a point of temporary silence.

Jesus looks across a short space and sees the Pharisees staring at him. Above the long beards they grow to display their esteemed age and venerable wisdom, he reads the anger and hatred on their faces. He can see the self-righteous rigidness in their crossed arms. They are stodgy and sullen and believe they are elite, far above the common people.

Jesus decides to pop their pompous balloons of self-importance.

He poses a simple question. It is a question that any of the uneducated peasants nearby could answer.

What do you think about the Christ? Whose son is he?

It takes no great learning for them to answer. Every Jewish child learns early that the Messiah will descend from David's family.

"The son of David," the Pharisees answer with patronizing scorn. *Every idiot knows this answer,* they imply. *How could you be so dumb to ask?*

You can see Jesus' eyebrows arch in mock surprise at their answer. He demonstrates not only considerable knowledge of Scripture, but playfulness as well when he quotes the first verse of Psalm 110. *The Lord said to my Lord . . .*

In true debating style, Jesus is laying the foundation for the question he will ask next. *If this is true—and of course it is because it is Scripture—how do you explain the contradiction? If the Messiah is David's son, why would David call him "Lord"?*

It is a fun way to publicly stump these self-righteous men who presume to sit in judgment on anyone they consider lesser than themselves.

And stump them it does. To the point that not one is able to say a word in reply. It stumps them so well, they dare not play debate games with him again.

The answer, had they humbled themselves to seek it from Jesus, is simple. It is the Messiah's glory that compels David to address his descendant as "Lord," because the Messiah's true father is God Himself.

But, of course, this is something the Pharisees cannot admit. Not when belief in their own abilities to uphold the law has transcended any true belief in God—or in the Messiah who has performed miracles in front of their very eyes.

If then David calls him 'Lord,' how can he be his son?"

No one could say a word in reply, and from that day on no one dared to ask him any more questions.

Matthew 22:41–46

4 9

The Price of Silver

Then one of the Twelve—the one called Judas Iscariot—went to the chief priests and asked, "What are you willing to give me if I hand him over to you?"

So they counted out for him thirty silver coins. From then on Judas watched for an opportunity to hand him over.

Matthew 26:14–16

WEDNESDAY WAS PROBABLY THE BEST DAY FOR JUDAS TO SLIP away from Jesus and the other disciples. It was the day Jesus chose to remain in Bethany, away from the temple, to rest and remain in prayer.

Judas, the keeper of the purse, could find any number of reasons to go back into the city alone. Perhaps he was sent to purchase the sacrificial lamb for the next day's Passover feast. So he goes and is unsuspected by his friends.

On a bright spring day Judas walks to the temple with darkness in his heart. The direction of the political winds is easy to detect. Everyone in power wants Jesus dead. Jesus himself has predicted he will be crucified within the next couple of days.

Judas easily foresees that the three years he has invested in following the Messiah will be wasted. Worse, if he is indicted as one of the followers, Judas himself might die.

He has made his decision. It is time to leave this sinking ship. And while he is jumping overboard, he might as well get what he can. Even better, if the religious authorities pay him to betray Jesus, they can't very well come back later and prosecute him as a follower.

Judas finds a gathering of chief priests, the men who head the temple rituals and administration, order and laws. It is not a formal gathering, where the Sanhedrin officially meet to try criminal cases. Instead, they are deep in discussions that must not be recorded by any scribe. Their priority issue, of course,

is this prophet from Galilee who threatens each of these areas of temple jurisdiction. He must be stopped. But he is too popular. If he is taken publicly, the people will riot. Pilate will send in his troops. How can he be taken in secret?

Judas approaches.

Is he calm and smug as he faces the most powerful men in Jerusalem? Apprehensive? Expecting to be treated as a hero?

To their great relief, Judas offers a solution. Yet, even they find it repugnant that this man is willing to betray his best friend. They could understand if Judas gave an ideological disagreement as his reason—heated passion, friends who have become enemies over fundamental beliefs—this they could almost respect.

But when they fail to mention a reward, Judas nakedly requests money. He is not a man deciding it is important to save Israel by stopping the rebel, but a base opportunist. He is someone selling himself as well as his best friend.

Their relief is mixed with scorn. Judas probably would have accepted five or ten pieces, but in contempt, as much of Judas as of Jesus, they offer thirty.

Thirty pieces of silver. It is the legal price of a slave.

Later they can calm their consciences by telling themselves that by purchasing Jesus like any other slave, there is some legality in handing him over to the Roman authorities.

Thirty pieces of silver. At this price, Judas is not joined in their cause and does not become an associate of the powerful and elite, as perhaps he had hoped. He is now a contemptible slave trader, a hireling.

There is irony, of course, that Jesus was paid for out of the temple treasury, with silver that had been marked for the purchase of sacrifices. And irony that Jesus, who took the role of servant for us all, was purchased for the price of a slave.

As for Judas, who will hang himself before Jesus is crucified, thirty pieces of silver is not only the price of slavery to greed and ambition and self-preservation, but the value of his own cheapened life.

A Man Carrying a Water Jar

MIDMORNING ON THURSDAY, JESUS AND THE DISCIPLES rest in the master's favorite garden, just outside the city—Gethsemane. The sun makes it a pleasant wait. Jesus and all but one of the disciples recline against the trunks of gnarled olive trees.

It is Judas who paces, filled with tension.

He is thirty pieces of silver richer, but there remains the problem of earning that silver. Somehow, he must arrange a time and location where the authorities can arrest Jesus.

This is not an easy matter. Worried about riots, the high priests have instructed Judas that it must be carried out in a private place.

Here in this garden, this morning, of course, would be perfect. But if Judas leaves now, there is no certainty that Jesus and the disciples will still be here when the religious authorities arrive.

No, Judas needs to know a place and location ahead of time. Especially because it will allow him to be among the disciples when the authorities appear, giving him a chance to remain unsuspected as the betrayer.

But, Judas keeps asking himself, *when and where will Jesus be at a prearranged place?*

Jesus sent Peter and John, saying, "Go and make preparations for us to eat the Passover."

"Where do you want us to prepare for it?" they asked.

He replied, "As you enter the city, a man carrying a jar of water will meet you. Follow him to the house that he enters, and say to the owner of the house, 'The Teacher asks: Where is the guest room, where I may eat the Passover with my disciples?'"

LUKE 22:8–12

When the solution strikes Judas, it is so obvious he smiles.

Of course! The Passover supper!

He hides his urgency as he walks toward Jesus.

"We must begin to prepare for the Passover supper," Judas says. "As you know, room is scarce in the city. Let me go ahead and find a place for the evening."

Jesus is silent.

"I am the keeper of the common purse," Judas continues, hoping his voice doesn't tremor. "Surely it is my responsibility to—"

Jesus shakes his head at Judas' question, but says nothing.

Judas steps away, face burning with shame and anger, assuring himself that a curt dismissal like this is justification for his decision. His renewed sense of alienation heightens his determination to carry through the betrayal.

Judas wanders away, thinking only thoughts of self-pity.

A half hour later, the call of trumpets rings through Jerusalem, signaling to the Jews that eating leavened bread must cease in preparation for the Passover.

Jesus rises from his comfortable position at the foot of the tree and calls for Peter and John. His voice, after the long silence, naturally draws the attention of the rest of the disciples. Judas moves closer, too.

"Rabbi?" Peter asks.

"Go and make preparations for us to eat the Passover," Jesus says. His tone holds sad resignation.

"Where do you want us to prepare for it?" John asks.

Judas leans forward, straining to hear the answer. His heart pounds and he swallows hard, as if this were the actual moment of betrayal. Now, he will get the answer he needs, and later he will find an excuse to slip away and deliver this information to the authorities.

Jesus will be defeated.

But Judas can scarcely believe what he hears. Jesus does not give a location but simply tells them to look for a man carrying a jar of water.

While Peter and John wonder at the vague instructions, Judas understands.

Carrying water was a woman's work, out of the ordinary for a man . . . and an extraordinarily simple way to be recognized by whomever Jesus sent. A man carrying a water jar would easily stand out from the crowd, especially if sent to meet Jesus' followers immediately after the call of trumpets.

Judas understands.

Jesus had already made arrangements for a room for the Passover supper—he must have planned this simple method of finding a man with a water jar as a way to keep the location unknown ahead of time.

Judas understands.

Jesus had not only foreseen his intentions but had taken steps to thwart him.

And Judas understands even more.

Jesus is in control. Judas is not.

The Passover Lamb

> The disciples left, went into the city and found things just as Jesus had told them. So they prepared the Passover.
>
> MARK 14:16

Temple sacrifices were not meant as a gift or appeasement to the mighty God of creation. ❧ The Hebrew word for sacrifice—korban—derived from the same root word that meant "to approach." ❧ The Jews believed that a person lived between the spiritual and physical worlds and because of this was caught between a battle of the dark desires of the flesh and the imprisoned soul's desire to reach God. A person

IT IS THURSDAY, THE DAY OF PASSOVER. YOU STAND with Peter and John in front of the massive Nicanor Gates inside the temple courts. Peter holds the Passover lamb for the meal tonight with Jesus. John waits patiently beside him.

Around you is a packed crowd of noisy pilgrims all preparing to celebrate the Passover feast that evening. Hear the bleating of lambs above the babble of the crowd. Smell the pungent aroma of fresh dung and human sweat in the afternoon heat.

On the other side of the tall, heavy doors, the Priest's Court is filling with hundreds upon hundreds of white-robed priests and Levites as they prepare for the afternoon ceremonies; this is the one day of the year when every temple priest is called to duty at the sacrificial altars.

When the priests finally open the gates, you, along with Peter and John and hundreds of other pilgrims, push ahead.

For some, it is their first sight of the altar. Not only is Passover different from the regular sacrifices because ordinary people participate in the killing, but it is one of the few yearly occasions when Israelite worshipers are allowed to enter the priests' inner domain.

The size of the altar is awesome enough to silence any pilgrim. Built on the same site on Mount Moriah where centuries earlier Abraham had bound his son Isaac for slaughter, the altar is a perfect square of stones and earth. Twice the height of a house, it has an ascent ramp leading to the top, where three fires burn. The largest—for burning sacrifices—is a pile of glowing, crackling wood taller than the priests who tend it with long metal tongs.

You see a line of priests all the way down the massive steps of the altar, from top to bottom, in a long double row that extends past the steps to the center of the court. Each priest has gone through a lengthy purification process of cleansing and ritual. They are ready for their sacred duty—the spilling of blood.

When the gates are closed behind you, a three-fold blast from the priests' silver trumpets echoes against the stones of the temple walls. There is a pause, like a heartbeat stopped. And then, like a heartbeat pulsing to life again, hundreds of Levites begin the ancient chant of the Hallel, Psalms 113 to 118.

"Praise the Lord!" the Levites call to you and the other pilgrims. The rich deepness of a symphony of men rolls across the inner court.

"Praise the Lord!" everyone chants in return.

constantly struggled—unsuccessfully—to overcome this contradiction. In bringing korban, the offering showed individuals what they deserved if God were to judge them.

❧ Yet, to the Jews, the God of creation was not an unforgiving ogre who demanded the death throes of an animal as a substitute punishment. Instead, he was a God of love, giving his people this sacrificial system as a means of restoring personal spiritual life. The sacrifice, if offered with true repentance, represented the death of the physical side, thus freeing the true self to connect with God and giving the spiritual side victory over the physical side.

❧ This victory, of course, was only temporary. As a person's darker desires constantly won

the battle, sacrifices were constantly needed—until Jesus, the perfect lamb, who made the ultimate sacrifice by accepting death on the cross. ℐ To his first followers—Jews of the first century A.D.—Jesus offered the path to God the Father, his Father. The victory was permanent and complete.

The Levites continue the verses of the psalms. You and the other pilgrims repeat the first line of each psalm. Every remaining line of each psalm you respond by singing "hallelujah."

As the chant rises and falls, the first pilgrims at the base of the altar begin to sacrifice the animals they have brought with them. The priest at the front of each line catches the blood of the dying animal in a golden bowl and passes the bowl to the priest behind him, receiving an empty bowl in return. The priest behind passes it back. And, like buckets of water in a fire brigade, each new bowl is passed up the long line of priests until the final priest throws the blood in a spray at the base of the great fire of the altar and passes that bowl back down again.

Now Peter and John move forward to make the Passover sacrifice. The lamb in Peter's arms begins to twist and struggle in panic as it smells fear and blood.

"This is the day the Lord has made," the Levites chant in the strange thunderous roar of men caught up in the vicarious taste of death. "Let us rejoice and be glad in it."

And the people around you shout in return. *Hallelujah.*

At the priest's feet, Peter kneels with John. With full weight on both hands, Peter presses the struggling lamb's fragile body against the floor of the court. The priest's flowing white robe at the corner of Peter's vision is soaked with blood.

O Lord save us. O Lord grant us success.

And the people around you shout in return. *Hallelujah.*

With one hand against the lamb's head and a knife in his other hand, John slashes through the quivered tendons of the lamb's neck to slit its throat. As the lamb thrashes, blood spurts against his sleeve and Peter's.

Blessed is he who comes in the name of the Lord.

And the people around you shout in return. *Hallelujah.*

Hosanna in the highest. Hosanna in the highest.

And the people around you shout in return. *Hallelujah.*

And then you realize why the shouting and chanting are so eerily familiar.

These triumphant cries—the cries over the dying lamb—are the same hallel cries that rang through the valley on Sunday as thousands cheered Jesus' journey through the gates of Jerusalem.

Who Is the Greatest?

JEWISH LAW SPECIFICALLY DICTATED THAT PILGRIMS AT Passover not sit but recline on their left elbow and side, leaving their right hands free to eat. With their heads near the table and their feet pointing back towards the ground, the position of the guests made it impossible to reach over them to serve dishes. So the upper two-thirds of the elongated, oval table would be surrounded by a horseshoe of cushions and the lower third would be left uncovered, a place for the Passover dishes to be placed within reach—unleavened bread, bitter herbs, radishes, and vinegar in a bowl.

As Jesus and the twelve disciples entered the upper chamber for the Last Supper, Jesus no doubt took the cushion held for the head of the table—on the left side of the open end of the horseshoe, it was the second cushion from the end.

We know from Scripture that John sat at the end cushion, immediately to the right of Jesus, below the Master's feet (otherwise John could not have leaned back against his Master, as described in John 13:23).

There was one other seat deemed significant—the position of highest honor—the cushion to the left of Jesus, just above him.

Who would sit there?

It is natural to assume that over their three years together, the disciples would have sorted themselves into some type of pecking order. Judas, keeper of the purse, would have been near the top. Strong, impetuous Peter would have been there too. And James and John, whom Jesus had invited along with Peter on the Mount of Transfiguration.

Although Scripture doesn't tell us what caused them to quarrel over who was the greatest, it is easy to guess that the seat of honor was the reason. It was open for grabs, and their competition for it was nakedly obvious.

How childish.

How utterly human.

For Jesus, how utterly sad. At this final gathering with his friends, he was forced to deal with an issue so petty. Worse, it went against everything he had been trying to teach them in their three years together.

When would they learn, Jesus must have wondered. And how?

He took that night to teach them, as the greatest teacher would—by example.

He showed them humility by washing their feet.

Just as later he showed them his love by dying on a cross.

The Last Supper

This is the body that
was broken,
Take and eat.
This is the blood shed
for many,
Take and drink—amen.
And it will cover you
And make you new—
oh Jerusalem.
I know we'll be together
Someday again,
Oh how I'll miss these
moments
With you my friends.
I know we'll be together
eternally,
And I will be there waiting—
come home to me.
Come home to me.

This is the body that
was broken,
Broken for us all.
Take and eat,
This is the blood shed
for many,
Take and drink—amen.
And when darkness comes,
Reach for me oh Israel,
oh Israel.
Come home to me.

❁ CINDY MORGAN

Show Us the Father

> Philip said,
> "Lord, show us the
> Father and that will
> be enough for us."
>
> Jesus answered,
> "Don't you know me,
> Philip, even after I
> have been among you
> such a long time? . . .
> Believe me when I say
> that I am in the Father
> and the Father is in
> me; or at least believe
> on the evidence of the
> miracles themselves."
>
> John 14:8–11

THE EVENING BEFORE THE CRUCIFIXION, AFTER JUDAS has departed the Passover supper, Jesus knows that little time remains to teach the eleven disciples. So, in the quiet of the upper chamber—as John records in his Gospel—Jesus begins to explain as clearly as possible who he is and where he is going.

Philip interrupts the passionate urgency of Jesus' voice by making the request we would all like to make in our moments of doubt. Show us the Father and that will be enough for us.

It is easy to understand the touch of exasperation in Jesus' reply. "Don't you know me, Philip, even after I have been among you such a long time?"

After all, in those three years, among the thirty-five miracles recorded in the Gospels, Jesus had turned water into wine, healed a man mute and possessed, commanded a storm to cease, and raised Lazarus from the dead. And Philip's eyes had seen the miracles. His tongue tasted the wine; his ears heard the mute man speak; his face felt the storm's lashing raindrops cease; his nose smelled the odor of Lazarus' burial clothes.

Sight, sound, touch, smell, and taste—Philip had ample proof. Yet that night during the Passover supper, he still requested confirmation of God's presence and existence.

Philip's request and the question Jesus asked him in reply, both show the pitiful limitations of our external senses. After all, we are so imprisoned by our frail mortal bodies, by gravity and by linear time, that we rarely recognize them as prison bars around our souls. Unlike Jesus, our perspective is narrowed by a minute span of years on a tiny planet lost in the mysteries of infinity.

In short, because of our limitations, miracles alone do not lead us to faith.

Yet listen to Jesus continue in a way that seems to directly contradict his first response to Philip.

"Believe me when I say that I am in the Father and the Father is in me, or at least believe on the evidence of the miracles themselves."

Why, then, if miracles do not lead to faith, would Jesus point Philip back to the miracles?

Because if we have faith, then his miracles do show us the One who superseded nature in the very act of creating it.

Philip wanted to approach Christ's miracles to receive faith, which was like expecting the cart to push the horse. God—who designed us—knows our frail bodies cannot perceive him.

Instead, when Philip turned to the miracles with faith, he was able to understand Jesus' divinity.

We, in turn, have the witnessed record of a man who walked the earth and worked the miracles that all of our senses can understand, including the greatest miracle of all—his resurrection.

We need to remember that while our eyes let us see the miracles, our faith gives us spiritual vision to believe in God.

Who Will Betray Him?

Simon Peter motioned to this disciple and said, "Ask him which one he means."

Leaning back against Jesus, he asked him, "Lord, who is it?"

JOHN 13:24–25

JOHN IS TO THE RIGHT OF JESUS AT THE PASSOVER TABLE. On the other side, to Jesus' left, Judas reclines in the place of honor. So when Jesus looks around the Passover table and declares that one will betray him, Judas is able to ask his question quietly while the other disciples babble in surprise and dismay.

"Surely, not I," he says, deliberately echoing the words of the others to avoid their attention. *How could Jesus know?*

The light in Jesus' eyes fragments into shards of pain. Although he is looking at Judas, he sees past him—into a night of utmost loneliness, a night with the depths of hell at his feet, a night with fires of torment licking at the edges of his soul.

Jesus does not answer immediately.

Judas holds his breath in silence.

After a moment Jesus answers softly, "Yes, it is you."

Judas recoils, waiting for Jesus to call the others down upon him. But Jesus bows his head and retreats into himself.

As the noise of conversation dies, Jesus speaks again.

"I am not referring to all of you," he says, troubled pain thickening his words. "I know the ones whom I have chosen."

One of

Jesus stares at the blood-red wine of the third cup. He absently lifts a piece of bread, then drops it—the actions of a man so deep in thought he has little realization what his hands do.

"This is to fulfill the Scriptures," he says, lifting his eyes to those around the table. "He who shares my bread has lifted up his heel against me. I am telling you now before it happens, so that when it does happen you will believe that I am He."

Jesus pauses. He wants to contrast the betrayer with those who do the opposite. "I tell you the truth, whoever accepts anyone I send accepts me. Whoever accepts me accepts the one who sent me."

Jesus' shoulders slump. His face softens with sad defeat. He knows the future and feels the pain of betrayal. "And I tell you the truth. One of you is going to betray me."

The repeated emphasis of this betrayal again throws the table conversation into excited disarray, Peter, directly across from John, motions for his friend to lean forward.

"Ask him which one he means," Peter urges.

John nods and leans back against Jesus.

"Lord, who is it?" John asks in a low voice.

Jesus begins to assemble a sop of unleavened bread wrapped around bitter herbs and meat from the Passover lamb.

"It is the one to whom I will give this piece of bread when I have dipped it in the dish."

Jesus dips the sop into a sauce of stewed fruit and hands it to Judas.

Obvious as the message is, John does not understand—Judas is in the place of honor, he is expected to receive the sop first.

Before John can ask Jesus to clarify his answer, Jesus dips another piece of bread into the sauce and hands it to the disciple next to Judas. John thinks Jesus is being deliberately vague . . . only later will John understand.

John gives Peter a silent shrug to indicate that the Master has not really answered.

Jesus dips more bread and although he does not speak loudly, John overhears.

"What you are about to do," Jesus tells Judas, "do quickly."

John misunderstands a second time, so inconceivable is it that Judas would be the betrayer. Judas, the one who worked hardest, the one trusted with the money. Jesus, it seems, is sending him out on an errand to buy something for the Passover feast or to give something to the poor.

So Judas of Iscariot, bread from the Master still held in his hand, rises and departs into the night—a night of utmost loneliness, a night with the depths of hell at his feet, a night with fires of torment licking at the edges of his soul.

going to

betray me

A Black Heart

> As soon as Judas
> took the bread,
> Satan entered
> into him.
>
> JOHN 13:27

KNOWING THAT JUDAS WAS THE KEEPER OF THE PURSE, we can guess that he was gifted with administrative skills. Jesus, in his wisdom, understood that when people are engaged in what suits them best, they are more likely to be content.

Yet each God-given aptitude has a potential dark side, because the areas closest to our hearts are the areas where temptations will test us the most.

This was true with Judas. Eventually, his honesty in caring for the money that belonged to the band of disciples became dishonesty. His love for money matters brought him to the cliff's edge where he could not resist temptation.

Yet, it is safe to say that Judas did not first follow Jesus because he foresaw the opportunity to rob from a meager collective purse.

If Judas' heart was in administration, perhaps early in Jesus' ministry he saw a chance to achieve power in an organization that was growing rapidly in status, reputation, and members. Its leader had solid credentials as a miracle worker. He was charismatic and extremely intelligent. Even more exciting, it was highly possible that he was, indeed, the long-awaited Messiah.

For an ambitious person like Judas, this appeared the perfect opportunity to get in on the ground floor of something impressive.

As the three years of ministry progressed, however, disillusionment set in. After feeding thousands from a few loaves of bread and some tiny fish, did Jesus take the opportunity to consolidate his power-base with the droves of astounded and impressed recruits? No, he gave a hard and almost repugnant lesson about eating the flesh of the Son of Man and drinking his blood (John 6:53). Followers deserted Jesus as if he had the very leprosy they had watched him cure.

With self-centered ambition, Judas could easily justify and nurture frustration.

At the transfiguration, did Jesus invite Judas? No, he took Peter and James and John.

With self-centered ambition, Judas could easily justify and nurture stung pride and anger.

Finally, in Jerusalem, Jesus announced that he expected to be crucified by week's end.

With self-centered ambition, Judas could easily justify and nurture thoughts of betrayal.

In Judas we see the danger of using a God-given gift for selfish gain.

Thoughts turned inward do not look upward. Judas, like any of us when we are focused solely on ourselves, found himself at the cliff's edge. From there it is far too easy to fall into the void of godlessness.

And from there it is far too easy for Satan to step in where God has been pushed aside.

self-centered

Can You Hear Me?

(Jesus prays in the garden)

Hey can you hear me?
Are you really out there?
Oh I am trapped in the cages
Of the scars I must bear.
And I can't tell and I can't speak,
I can't even repeat what it is.

Hey can you see me,
See these hollowing eyes?
Don't you think something is
        missing
In my calm peaceful smile?
But I can't tell and I can't speak,
I can't even repeat what it is.

Can you hear me,
Hear the sound of my pain?
Can you hear me,
Hear the words I don't say?

Hey, what's your problem?
Can't you hear what I said?
I am here drowning in sorrow
While you sleep on your beds.
And I can't tell and I can't speak,
I can't even repeat what it is, oh

I get down on my knees
And I cry to You
Oh, Lord give me all Your strength;
Help me make it through.
I reach out to You.

O can You hear me; hear me, yeah.

✿ CINDY MORGAN

Drops of Blood

Then he said to
them, "My soul is
overwhelmed with
sorrow to the point of
death. Stay here and
keep watch with me."

Going a little farther,
he fell with his face
to the ground and
prayed, "My Father,
if it is possible,
may this cup be
taken from me.
Yet not as I will,
but as you will."

MATTHEW 26:38–39

WATCH THE ENTRANCE TO THE GARDEN OF GETHSEMANE. Upon entering with his disciples, Jesus pauses—not from fear of the twisted shadows of shrubs and olive trees, innocent in daylight yet sinister in darkness, for even at night the garden is a sanctuary, a place of peace and beauty.

No, Jesus pauses among his disciples because he has faltered under the weight of sorrow and desolation.

His voice is low and hoarse: "Sit here, while I go over there and pray."

Without question, the disciples obey. It was usual for Jesus to take time alone with his Father.

"Pray that you will not fall into temptation," Jesus says. Utter loneliness overwhelms him. He does what any man would do—he turns to his friends.

He places one hand on Peter's shoulder. With his other, he lightly touches James and John, the sons of Zebedee. These are the three men closest to him, the three who witnessed his transfiguration, who stood beside him when he raised the daughter of Jairus from the dead.

They follow Jesus deeper into the garden where he shares his troubles with them, drawing a deep breath to find strength.

"My soul," he says, "is overwhelmed to the point of death."

He turns to them, outlined by the moonlight of the garden night. "Stay here and keep watch with me."

He does not beg. The need is in his voice. The obvious agony of his soul terrifies them. This is the man who calmed the storm, who walked across water. What thing of horror can bend him to this point of defeat?

Terror mutes them.

Jesus walks away, but not so far that they are unable to see him collapse on his face as he kneels. When he prays aloud, his voice carries to them.

"My Father, if it is possible, may this cup be taken from me"—a human plea.

"Yet, not as I will, but as you will"—divine submission.

Both of his natures cry out in that prayer. Body. And soul.

Both natures agonize in the contradiction of a perfect duality, submitting to the humiliation of death. It is the spiritual anguish of a single star shrinking to oblivion in an eternal night of infinite black. It is a physiological anguish so great that his body responds by constricting the vessels near the skin.

Drops of blood fall from his brow.

Only later, after the resurrection, when Peter and the sons of Zebedee truly know that Jesus is divine, are they able to look back on this moment and understand that his pain was far greater than any pain man had ever suffered.

Fallen man is born with the certainty of death's future claim. Body and soul are fused at the beginning to be torn apart at the end.

Jesus, however, was born into this world without the selfishness of the body's sins to dim the spirit's awareness of God. For him, unlike any other man, there was no need for death to free his soul from a decaying prison of flesh.

To man, death must be accepted because it is inevitable.

To Jesus it was the ultimate miscarriage of justice.

Yet when the soldiers and chief priests approached with swords and clubs, he did not wait for them to reach him. He stood from his prayers and walked toward them.

Death was his choice.

Made for us.

❧

The Kiss

Now the betrayer had arranged a signal with them: "The one I kiss is the man; arrest him."

Going at once to Jesus, Judas said, "Greetings, Rabbi!" and kissed him.

Jesus replied. "Friend, do what you came for."

MATTHEW 26:48–50

IN THE NIGHT, THE MEN WITH TORCHES AND SWORDS and clubs approach Gethsemane. Judas breaks away from the crowd and quickly crosses the short gap to reach Jesus and the disciples. Illuminated by the torches behind him, Judas makes an unerring line for Jesus.

With both hands raised in enthusiastic greeting, he calls loudly for the benefit of the men with the torches and swords and clubs who follow. "Hail, Rabbi!"

Judas brings a hand down on each of Jesus' shoulders and hugs him closely, kissing first one side of his face, then the other.

"Judas," Jesus says, "are you betraying me with a kiss?"

The sad question needed no answer.

Judas had anticipated that moment with satisfaction, expecting Jesus to react with anger or shock. Either would have allowed Judas to spill his bitterness and tell Jesus he had been a fool to forsake the chance of becoming *the* messiah to conquer the Romans. And an equal fool to slight Judas in as many ways as he had. It would have allowed Judas to remind Jesus of all that he had sacrificed and how he had worked hardest of the followers to please Jesus.

Yes, anger and shock would have justified the kiss of betrayal.

Instead, Jesus' resignation and sadness are a heart blow to Judas. In one horrifying moment, he realizes the full magnitude of what he has done—he is overwhelmed by desperate shame, like a straying husband, who before the sin enjoys the temptation and shivers of false expectations, only to see clearly after the sin the harlot's wrinkles and painted face.

Judas, are you betraying me with a kiss?

Would that Judas could have turned and sent the soldiers and chief priests away with their torches and swords and clubs. Would that he could have fallen at Jesus' feet and begged for forgiveness. Would that instead of this moment it could have been any moment along the dusty Galilean roads, when the sun shone brightly and the future was the hope he had carried in the presence of Jesus.

But it is this moment. The men bear torches and swords and clubs—the men Judas has led to his Master's garden. Much as black remorse crushes him, Judas cannot change what he has done.

"Friend," Jesus says. Judas hears love in his Master's voice. "Do what you came for."

Judas is too stricken to reply.

And the men with the torches and swords and clubs push past him to take his beloved Master away.

The Only Way

(the soldiers arrest Jesus)

Here you come
With your swords and clubs,
Thinking that
You're gonna fight today.
Small applause for your
Rebel cause, cause my
Feet are walking by another way.
Flames and torches
Marching forward to fate,
Don't you know . . .
I am the light,
I am the truth,
I am the voice
That will lead you;
I am the peace,
I am the love,
I am the way,
I'm the only way, oh . . .

Flowing robes in a judge's pose,
But their evidence is all full
   of holes.
Pilate's washing his bloody hands,
But he just can't get 'em clean.
Crucify Him, Crucify Him today—
   don't you know . . .
I am my Father's son,
It is as you say
Lord, Thy will be done.
Drink the cup, drink it up,
Drink the blood, drink it up,
Drink the cup for the children's
   sake.
I'm the only way.
Don't you know? . . .

❁ CINDY MORGAN

A Field of Blood

When Judas,
who had betrayed
him, saw that Jesus
was condemned,
he was seized
with remorse. . . .
Then he went away
and hanged himself.

MATTHEW 27:3–5

AFTER THE BETRAYAL, JUDAS BECAME A MAN WILD WITH conflicting emotions—despair, horror, regret, and shame. All of it because of what he had done and could not undo. Standing there, haggard and desperate in front of the chief priests, trying to take the selfishness out of his act by returning the thirty pieces of silver, he was a man almost insane from guilt.

To the priests, he was an intrusion, a reminder of their own shame. They treated him with scorn, the contempt of a user for the used, and sent him away.

Thirty pieces of silver fell on the marble floor, and with a deep groan Judas rushed away, fleeing from himself.

Lungs wheezing to the point of exhaustion, thigh muscles burning with fatigue, he ran . . . stumbled . . . fell and ran on beyond the city walls to the darkness of the valley outside Jerusalem. When he could run no longer, his aching legs drove him to keep climbing up the jagged rocks. Finally, high on the hill where the Kidron and Hinnom valleys merge, he understood . . .—there was no place to go. No matter how dark the night, no matter how far from Jerusalem and Jesus he ran, there was no place on earth where he could forget who he was and what he had done.

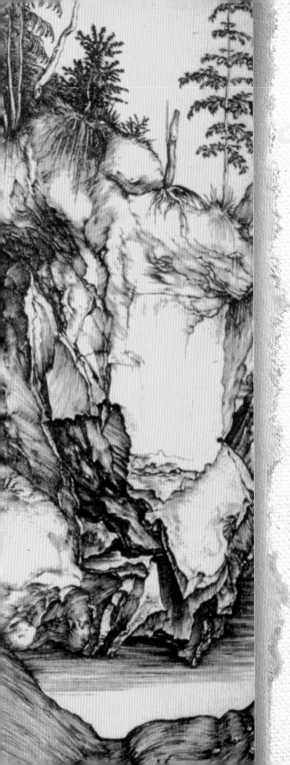

Then he spied a tree outlined against the cold moonlight, old and gnarled, rooted in the windswept soil of a rock at the edge of the chasm.

With a solution in sight, he calmed himself and removed the girdle of his tunic—the girdle that had carried thirty pieces of silver. Once the girdle was fastened to a branch, he hung it around his neck and threw himself out into the night.

There was no one to mourn his dark, lonely death.

Gone was the intoxication of temptation, the delightful tremble of false expectations. Gone was the glamour of sin.

On a horrible night both Peter and Judas betrayed their Lord and Master.

One returned to Jesus. One did not.

One repented, one did not.

One found peace. The other? A field of blood.

Devil Man

(Judas, the betrayer)

Give me the money,
Give me the gold,
Dirty little palms
And a heart that's cold, yeah.
A kiss of the serpent,
A bite of the fruit,
You can keep the knowledge;
I just want the loot,
Want the loot . . .
I just want the loot, yeah.
I'm making deals
With a mighty bad hand;
Fishing on a boat
That is sinking in sand.
And I'm messing into things
That I never should have,
And I'm making plans
With the Devil Man.

Sneaking through the dark
Like a vigil in black,
I kiss you on the cheek
Then I stab you in the back, yeah.
Cause what I didn't know
Is what I didn't know;
The hammer cracked and the blood
it flowed, yeah.
And I wish I could take it back,
hey, but
Hanging from my neck
From a dirty piece of wood.
I'm known as the betrayer—
Buried in a field of blood,
In a field of blood, hey.

✿ CINDY MORGAN

The Sound of a New Day

> Then Peter
> remembered the
> word the Lord
> had spoken to him:
> "Before the rooster
> crows today, you will
> disown me three times."
> And he went outside
> and wept bitterly.
>
> LUKE 22:61-62

IN JESUS' DAY, THREE YEARS OF TRAVELING TOGETHER on foot meant endless hours of conversation to fill the unhurried time—shared laughter, astonishment, sorrow, disappointment, and anger during events so incredible they have been told and retold for nearly twenty centuries. In today's society, where the hectic pace of work and play and the distractions of technology tend to cocoon each of us, it is hard to comprehend how closely all of this would knit a friendship.

Yet close as the friendship was between Peter and Jesus, one denied the other, even when forewarned that it would happen.

It took place in the Palace of Annas the High priest, a luxurious building located on the hillside of upper Jerusalem. An outer court, inner court, and dozens of rooms were connected by mazes of corridors. On that cold spring night a coal fire burned in the center of the inner courtyard, throwing a small glow of light on the bearded men who talked in excited tones about the capture of a rebel messiah. Jesus, in an audience chamber somewhere in the depths of the palace, faced his accusers alone.

The Synoptic Gospels tell us that Peter sat down among the servants at the fire; John's Gospel tells us he

stood up. In short, Peter was restless and uninvolved in the stories around the fire. This attracted the attention of the maid who had first admitted him to the circle. The firelight was uncertain; so was she. "Weren't you also with that Nazarene, Jesus?"

What went through Peter's mind as he readied his answer? Did he tell himself that by incriminating himself he would not help Jesus? Did he reason that, worse, he might be brought forward to testify against Jesus and thus actually harm his master's cause? Did he tell himself that the woman—after all, she was only a woman in a time when women were regarded as second-class citizens—had no moral or legal right to his confession?

Peter justified, then denied.

There is something peculiar about human nature. In almost inverse proportion, the more off-kilter our stance, the more strenuously we defend it—justification requires further justification for the self-deception to survive.

We can understand why Peter, with every additional denial, added more bricks to build a higher wall of defense— a wall, the cock's crow should have reminded him, that was being built not between him and his accusers but between him and Christ.

At that point, however, Peter's attention was not focused on Jesus but on himself and his scramble to keep safe. Pacing back and forth in the night, worrying about his deception, the first cries of the rooster did not even brush his conscious thoughts.

In Peter we see ourselves. Anything we truly want we justify. Pride pushes us to cling to the justification. And selfishness—choosing our will against the will of God—deafens us to his warning calls.

For Peter, it took the second crowing of a rooster to penetrate his self-absorption. (God will not stop trying to reach us!) Once Peter's heart was pierced—to his credit—he allowed the bricks to crumble and the wall to fall. Remorse took him away from self-justification back to his friendship with a man about to die for his sins.

Peter's story raises a simple question. Are there walls in our lives that need to crash with the sound of a new day—a day of God's forgiveness?

The Loving Kind

(Peter's song to Jesus)

Happy as a little child, yeah
Walking by the shepherd's side, oh
How I know You,
How You know me.
Your words are like peace and truth,
Like flowers kissed by morning dew,
    yeah
How I know You,
And how You know me, oh Lord.
I don't know why you love me,
Oh Lord it's such a mystery;
All I can say,
All I can find, You're the loving kind—
The loving kind.
When I fall and when I stay,
Your love it captures me always.
All I can see, all I can find,
You're the loving kind, the loving kind.
Sitting in a courtyard still,
They all come marching for the kill;

They don't know You,
But how I know You,
I got scared, I ran away;
The rooster crowed,
    my faith it swayed.
How I know You,
But I denied You, Oh Lord.
Lord, I believe in You
Though I have deceived You.
Thank God that forgiveness is
    reigning again,
Thank God that forgiveness
    is reigning again.
I don't know why you love me
    like You do,
All I know is You're the loving kind . . .
    the loving kind.

❁ CINDY MORGAN

They Wanted Jesus to Die

*I*T WAS CERTAIN THAT JESUS WOULD NOT RECEIVE A FAIR trial the night he was captured.

Caiaphas, the high priest, was overcome with fear—Jesus' popularity threatened to spark all the Jews into suicidal rebellion against the Romans. Yet when he came to trail, Judea's roman governor, Pontius Pilate, saw so little of this danger that he did his best to release Jesus, who, after all, showed no interest in establishing an earthly kingdom.

No, this lone peasant from Galilee was not a threat to the majority of the people, but to a small minority—the entire spectrum of established religious and political parties.

The *Pharisees* were among those who taught law, as based on the commandments of Moses and layers of interpretations they derived from those commandments. Not all Pharisees were ungodly, but the ones most threatened by Jesus (and the most vocal about it) were ritualistic, self-righteous, hypocritical, and rigid in thought.

For example, when Jesus taught that the law could be summed up in two commandments—love God and love your neighbor as yourself—it banished all the carefully

Then one of them, named Caiaphas, who was high priest that year, spoke up. "You know nothing at all! You do not realize that it is better for you that one man die for the people than that the whole nation perish."

JOHN 11:49, 50

constructed series of rules the Pharisees has laid upon the people. And since the Pharisees taught that God's grace extended only to those who kept the laws, they were outraged that Jesus contradicted them by teaching that God was merciful to all. To the Pharisees, the more people who followed Jesus, the more their own authority was undermined.

The *Sadducees* also taught the law but did not believe in a resurrection (Mark 12:18–27). This group consisted of wealthy, elite Jews (mainly of Jerusalem) who focused their efforts on the administration of the temple—an excellent source of revenues. Though small in number, during Jesus' time they had considerable religious and political influence. When Jesus disrupted their lucrative income from the temple markets, it became clear he was a threat to more than their religious beliefs.

The *Herodians* were a political party in favor of Roman rule. They wanted to see Herod, who ruled Galilee, also replace the roman governor of Judea. The religious authorities in Judea's Jerusalem, however, feared that Herod would strip them of their powers at the first chance. To the Herodians, the more earthly authority Jesus assumed, the less chance that Herod would gain control of Judea. It showed the extent of their mutual desperation when the Herodians joined with the Pharisees in attacking Jesus (Matthew 22:16).

The Great Sanhedrin, which was the ruling body of the Jews at that time, drew from the wealthy and intellectual and scholarly men of all these parties. In the end, it served all of their best interests to see Jesus dead.

The Great Sanhedrin

DURING HIS FIRST TRIAL, JESUS FACED THE GREAT SANHEDRIN, a tribunal ruling body of the legal system—Jews who had authority on all local matters except death. At least twenty-three members were needed for a quorum.

Altogether, Israel had three tribunals. The lowest tribunal—consisting of three judges—held limited jurisdiction and existed in towns with a population of less than 120 males. The next highest tribunal—for larger centers—consisted of twenty-three judges, whose authority, while somewhat limited, did give them jurisdiction over some capital causes. Finally, the seventy men of the highest tribunal, Jerusalem's Great Sanhedrin, presided over all matters and met in the temple's Chamber of Hewn Stones, under the direction of the seventy-first man, the chief priest, called Nasi, prince. There were no greater powers of Jewish authority in Israel. Although the Romans did not permit these ruling bodies to carry out the death sentence, they were still empowered to judge in those cases.

Unlike modern North American juries, which are appointed to represent a cross-section of society, the members of these tribunals were selectively appointed to guarantee a consistent outlook on how and why justice should be dispensed.

No man, in any tribunal, was ordained to office without approval of three tribunal judges, and at least one of those three had to be able to trace a chain of ordination, generation by generation, back to Moses himself. Appointments into the Great Sanhedrin were made by members of the Great Sanhedrin tribunal, choosing from lower tribunals or from disciples who formally sat in the temple and watched its proceedings.

Thus, all of these men had a vested interest in maintaining the status quo and their own high positions in society. It was these men whom Jesus faced during the long, dark night before his crucifixion.

Show Me a Miracle

> When Herod saw Jesus, he was greatly pleased, because for a long time he had been wanting to see him.
>
> LUKE 23:8

HEROD SITS ON HIS THRONE. A HANGOVER HAS PUT HIM in a foul mood. As Caiaphas rattles off a string of accusations against Jesus, Herod curses himself for having mixed wine and beer in such large amounts the night before. For any reason other than Jesus, Herod would have sent this delegation away.

The high priest's complaints are tiresome and predictable. Herod motions him silent.

"Bring in your prisoner," Herod says with a groan. "I'm quite familiar with all your complaints."

Too familiar by far. It was all these rabbis did, complain. Unhappy unless everyone shared their misery. *Parasitic, Pharisaic fools*, Herod thinks.

As he waits, Herod eases his throat by drinking red wine from a goblet, hoping the alcohol will set his blood coursing at this early hour.

The guards escort Jesus to the throne. Herod is not impressed by the man's size or his looks. *This* is the famous prophet who has stirred up so much trouble?

"Well," Herod finally says, hiding his initial disappointment. "I've been wanting to see you for some time."

He continues in a friendly tone. "I have heard of your exploits for years. The miracle healings, stories about fish and loaves and feeding the thousands. Truly amazing. I actually sent soldiers out looking for you. But not to harm you . . . despite what you might have heard about John the Baptist and his unfortunate death. After all, *he* never performed a single miracle . . ."

All this talk scratches Herod's throat. He drinks deeply from the goblet and sighs. "Would you grace us with a miracle? Right now? Nothing spectacular. It's early, and I wouldn't want you to tax yourself too much on my behalf."

Caiaphas and the other Jews watch with dread—they fear a miracle.

Herod and his soldiers crave new entertainment—they hope for a miracle.

As for Jesus, he merely closes his eyes, as if lost in deep thought.

"Come on," Herod cajoles. "These great religious leaders want you dead. Give us one miracle, and you will be released."

Jesus opens his eyes. Herod sees pity in that gaze. Pity for Herod. It bothers him that Jesus realizes he can find no enjoyment in life.

"Listen," Herod snaps. "I am offering you freedom. Show me a sign from God, and I'll bow down before you . . . and Him. One miracle is all I need. Turn a sword into a snake. Or make the ropes fall from your wrists. I'll let you go."

Jesus only smiles sadly.

Caiaphas clears his throat. "Noble Tetrarch, there is good reason he will not perform any miracles. He cannot. He is a hoax. A false prophet. You are well within your rights to have him stoned."

"Don't tell me what my rights are." Herod focuses his irritation on the chief priest. "Word of this failure to perform a miracle will get to the people. They will all stop following him. He doesn't need to be dead to lose his power."

Unspoken—and both of them know it—is Herod's legitimate fear of stirring up more trouble by killing another popular prophet. John the Baptist brought trouble enough.

"The Sanhedrin has found him guilty," Caiaphas says. "Surely that—"

"Take him back to Pilate. Continue the trial with him where you left off."

"Pilate?" Caiaphas is surprised. And worried. Pilate already refused to condemn Jesus. "Surely you cannot mean—"

"Silence! Push me farther and I will acquit this man immediately."

Caiaphas almost protests but thinks better of it as Herod carefully holds his goblet to step down from the throne and approach Jesus.

"If you can't perform a miracle, talk," Herod says. "Give us one of your famed parables."

Jesus' steady, silent gaze has strength that Herod cannot understand. Herod's usual insecurities arise and this angers him.

"Obviously you are too good for us," Herod says sarcastically. He removes his elegant robe and drapes it over Jesus' shoulders.

"Guards," Herod calls, "your king! Worship him. Then take him to Pilate."

Herod's guards pounce on the opportunity for crude sport. They blow trumpets in Jesus' ears. They drop to their knees in front of him with mock bows. They taunt him with vulgar comments about his ancestry.

Not once does Jesus show any sign of discomfort. He is so dignified, the laughter begins to die.

"Enough!" Herod says, finding the victory empty. "On your way."

The guards begin to push Jesus forward.

"Wait!" Herod calls. The procession stops.

"This water," Herod says, holding his goblet high. "Turn it to wine!"

Herod shakes the goblet as if a great force were taking hold of it. Seconds later, with the goblet a few inches above his mouth so that everyone can see the red contents, he pours the remainder of it into his mouth.

"Look, look," Herod laughs. "The water has become wine. A miracle!"

Moments later, when all are gone, Herod leans against the throne in defeat. Fat and wheezing, weary of exploring every luxury and sin with less satisfaction each passing year, he does not feel like a king. Why, with everything a man could ask for, does he feel there is so little to make life worthwhile?

How he had hoped to believe.

The Whipping Pillar

Then Pilate
took Jesus and
had him flogged.

JOHN 19:1

PILATE WATCHED THE SOLDIERS GATHERED AROUND
the whipping pillar as they began to strip Jesus. Pilate
knew what to expect. During his long career he had often
been among enlisted soldiers who engaged in these ancient
barbaric customs—games of mockery that followed after a
criminal had been whipped into a bloody froth.

One soldier already held a purple robe. Another had
gathered thorn branches and was weaving them into a
crown to force upon Jesus' forehead. From the vulgar
banter Pilate overhead, these soldiers found it humorous
that this tall, naked figure claimed to be king. They would
savage him for it, and in so doing vent their hatred for
the Jews, a conquered people who refused to play the
role of the conquered.

The other soldiers bent Jesus over the waist-high
pillar. A shallow channel had been gouged into the ground
below to drain blood. Flies collected on the small pools
of red that lay stagnant from the earlier whippings of two
convicted robbers.

Two burly men stood ready on each side of the pillar,
each holding whips of leather strands woven around
dozens of small shards of pottery. They waited for a
signal from the governor.

Pilate told himself he was letting an innocent man be whipped for a good reason. He hoped the intense pain of the scourging would force Jesus to defend the accusations against him. Pilate hoped, too, that once he showed a bloody, beaten man to the crowd—especially a beaten Jew to a crowd of Jews—that a collective pity would satiate their lust for his death.

Pilate nodded.

Soldiers kicked Jesus' legs apart, to expose all parts of his body equally.

One man with the whip grinned at the other before drawing his arm back. With a grunt of effort, he flung the whip down, cracking the thongs of leather against Jesus' back. It sounded like a length of bone snapping against stone.

As he pulled the whip away, his companion aimed lower and lashed savagely from the other side. Shards of pottery raked Jesus' buttocks and curled around the inside of his thighs.

Incredibly, Jesus did not cry out.

His silence spurred both men into an enthusiastic attack of alternating whips that carved instant rivers of blood across his shoulders and ribs and legs.

Pilate kept waiting for the man to cry out. Instead, it was Pilate who broke.

"Enough!" he barked.

Pilate turned his back as the soldiers swarmed in behind the two with the robe and the crown of thorns. His ears could not block out the jeers of their taunts . . . nor the thuds of their blows against Jesus' face.

Christ's punishment for our sins had just begun.

The Whipping

Oh they mocked Him,
and they beat Him.
They pressed a crown of thorns
Upon His head.
And He was bleeding
As He was pleading
For the lives of those who
Spit on Him—they screamed
Crucify Him, crucify Him.
Now who are you, you filthy Jew
To say you'll save us,
Oh and take us and
Forgive us of our sins?
Pain so thick and dull,
Marching to the skull.

❀ CINDY MORGAN

Daughters of Jerusalem

> A large number
> of people followed
> him, including women
> who mourned and
> wailed for him. Jesus
> turned and said to
> them, "Daughters of
> Jerusalem, do not
> weep for me; weep for
> yourselves and your
> children. For the time
> will come when you
> will say, 'Blessed
> are the barren
> women. . . .'"
>
> LUKE 23:27–29

UPON HIS ENTRANCE INTO JERUSALEM ON PALM SUNDAY, Jesus had wept over the women of Jerusalem. Now, as he neared the place of his death, the women in the crowd of followers wept for him.

The beam of lumber weighed only thirty pounds. Normally, a man who had earned a living as a carpenter would not find this too much of a load. But Jesus' muscular body had been ripped from whips. He had suffered pain so great it sucked the breath from his lungs and left him in physical shock. He had lost much blood and was on the verge of unconsciousness from thirst.

What probably tore most at the women's hearts was Jesus' struggle to continue stumbling up the road.

Falling and bearing the beatings silently, somehow he got to his feet one more time. Again and again . . . with the cross still on his back. It was as if something was driving him to reach Golgotha.

And so the women wept.

Yet when Simon took the cross and Jesus was physically able to respond to the women, he turned away their sympathy. He told them there would come a day when the barren woman would be considered blessed. He said terrible things were ahead for the daughters of Jerusalem.

Did they stare at him in amazement and bewildered disbelief? Infertility was a curse. The woman who did not bear her husband a child was looked down on by all other women; was in danger of being replaced by another wife, and, married or not, faced an impoverished and lonely old age once widowed.

Only a few decades later, of course, Jesus' words were fulfilled. When the Romans laid siege on Jerusalem—as the historian Josephus reports—desperate, frenzied mothers went so far as to roast and eat their own children. Perhaps some of the very women who wept for Jesus faced those horrible days, and likely they remembered his strange warning.

Yet Jesus firmly rejected their pity for a much more important reason than the fate he foresaw for the daughters of Jerusalem—their pity was misplaced. Those who merely saw the man, the fallen prophet, were those who failed to see his kingdom beyond, to see the reason for it all.

Jesus drove himself to his feet again and again because he had accepted the task that awaited him at Golgotha. Much more than the thirty pounds of rough-hewn lumber on his back, he carried the great need forced upon him by all the selfish desires and actions that separate all of us from God. His agony, exhaustion, and certain death were not payment for anything he had done wrong, but for what we have done wrong.

It is easy to weep when we see Jesus with the cross. But those are tears he does not want.

He does not want us to cry for his agony. He wants us to cry for our sins.

He wants us to ask forgiveness.

Carrying the Cross

> A certain man from Cyrene, Simon, the father of Alexander and Rufus, was passing by on his way in from the country, and they forced him to carry the cross.
>
> MARK 15:21

SIMON OF CYRENE—A JEW FROM THE SEAPORT WEST of Egypt's Alexandria—was not just another onlooker, following the soldiers as they drove Jesus and the two criminals toward Golgotha. He was on his own journey, coming into the city as the procession headed out, unaware until meeting the group that a centurion was about to order him to take a thirty-pound beam of lumber from an exhausted and bloody Jesus. Unaware that he was about to walk back out into the countryside on a brief journey to be recorded as long as history exists.

It is not so curious that the centurion recruited Simon, probably by tapping him on the shoulder with his spear, as Romans soldiers did to force citizens of occupied countries to obey orders. After all, it was a feast day following the Passover. Travel on this day—while not forbidden by Jewish law—was unusual. A solitary figure, Simon undoubtedly struck the immediate notice of the centurion.

Nor is it curious that Simon accepted the task without protest. Roman soldiers had a right to force any citizen to carry a load for up to a mile. With twelve soldiers guarding Jesus and the two criminals, Simon surely knew that resistance was not only futile, but dangerous.

What is curious, however, is that Simon of Cyrene was coming *in* from the country. If he was just arriving in Jerusalem as a pilgrim, something must have kept him from celebrating the Passover the night before. And since he had missed the Passover, why hurry into the city before it was stirring on a feast day? On the other hand, if he did celebrate the Passover in Jerusalem the night before, what beckoned him out from the city so early that he was already returning?

Either way it is safe to conclude that Simon's mind was focused on greater concerns than the unexpected, unsought, and highly inconvenient burden placed on him because of Jesus.

After accepting the cross, Simon had two choices: he could carry the cross, stare at the ground, and ignore Jesus—or he could set aside his resentment and make the best of a bad situation.

It seems he chose to resist resentment. Eyes lifted from the ground, he would have seen Jesus tell the daughters of Jerusalem not to weep for him but for themselves. He would have seen this beaten, blood-crusted man calmly accept the jeers of the crowd. Perhaps he stayed to watch soldiers drive spikes into Jesus' hands and feet. Perhaps he heard Jesus forgive the criminal on the cross. And most certainly, either at the cross or back in the city, Simon witnessed the three hours of darkness that covered the land, heard of the temple curtain torn in half.

Is it not also likely that Simon and Jesus talked to each other during that brief journey? Enough for us to guess that Simon had reason later to ask onlookers why the man had been condemned to crucifixion? Enough that once news of the empty tomb spread, Simon might have sought Jesus' followers to learn more about the man whose cross he had carried?

After all, from Mark's description of Simon, it seems the man from Cyrene did not simply forget the cross. If this had been only a brief encounter, Mark probably would not have added that Simon was the father of Alexander and Rufus (perhaps the same men mentioned in Acts 13:1), as if through Simon, those two sons came to believe in Jesus. We can guess that Mark did come to know Simon—and the simplest reason for this is because Simon came to know Jesus.

Yet, until the morning of the crucifixion, Simon had not been looking for Jesus. Strong and independent, Simon had his own business to attend to that morning. But the unexpected burden took his heart and thoughts off his own concerns and led him toward Jesus.

The cross Simon bore became a blessing.

And our burdens? Our crosses?

Will we stare at the ground and carry them resentfully?

Or will we learn from Simon, to walk with Jesus and allow our burdens to lead us closer to him?

Crucifixion

THIS IS HOW YOU WOULD DIE IF YOU WERE CRUCIFIED.
You would carry your upright beam to the site of execution. At thirty or forty pounds, this lumber is a bearable weight, except you are weak from the blood you have lost to the whips that slashed your back. You feel nearly naked as you walk past jeering crowds.

Perhaps, though, you are not aware of this pain or agony because you know what lies ahead. And dread from that knowledge far outweighs anything else you feel.

At the place you are to die, you watch as soldiers position the upright beam in the ground. They do not care about your fears. They tell jokes. Comment on the crowd. They wiggle the beam back and forth, filling the hole with dirt until it no longer moves—as if they are merely positioning a post for a fence. When they are satisfied, they turn their attention to you.

Another beam is set upon the ground. Nearby are sacks of provisions for the soldiers. They expect to be near the cross for some time, to guard against anyone helping you down. They will eat to satisfy their hunger as you die. They have seen this hundreds of times. Your groans and screams will not dull their appetite.

Now you are forced onto your back. If you resist, the soldiers will kick you brutally and slam you with their spears—but they will not kill you, that would be too merciful.

They lay you across the beam with your arms extended. You are grateful for the merciful Jewish tradition that allows a nearby woman to offer you a cup of strong wine mixed with myrrh. You drink it greedily, and the drugged wine begins to deaden your sensations. But when the hammer is lifted, your bladder weakens, perhaps empties, with renewed fear. Your moment has arrived. No amount of myrrh and wine can protect you now.

Several long, sharp nails are driven into your left hand, then the right, pinning your arms to the wood. Some of the hammer blows miss the spike and shatter bones in your fingers. The soldiers laugh. You know it could be worse. If the executioner had little skill or time, he would simply pound the nails halfway up the flesh of your forearm, confident that eventually your body weight would tear your arm's soft flesh until the bones of your wrist met the nails and arrested the slow agonizing, downward slide of the body.

Now you are secured to the cross-piece, helpless as soldiers use ropes to draw you upward. They bind the cross-piece to the upright beam with rope or nails. Your feet are barely off the ground.

At this point the soldiers are far from finished. If they left you hanging in this manner, death would arrive too quickly—from suffocation as your body's unsupported weight pulled down against your lungs.

So the soldiers turn your lower body sideways and push your legs upward. They know your large thigh muscles will almost immediately knot and cramp without any prospect of relief that comes from stretching. The soldiers drive spikes through each of your ankles, splintering bone.

You cannot scream, such is the pain. Your brain is flooded with the agonies searing through the different parts of your body. Flies settle on your wounds and eyes and nose to torment you.

Yet the real pain has not yet begun.

Left alone in this private hell, you will

choose the lesser agony of hanging from the nails driven into your hands simply because it is unbearable to place any weight on the fragmented bones of your ankles. You will begin to suffocate. Your lungs will strain for the sweetness of air until your throat rattles against the choking of your diaphragm, unable to push for one more gasp.

Your will to live is an unreasoning desperate creature; it ignores your wish to die. So you fight for air and push downward on those cramping thigh muscles, pushing your weight on the iron spikes in your ankles. Broken bone grates against broken bones, an unspeakable white-hot knife thrust of pain, a pain that robs you of the very breath you seek.

When you can no longer endure this pain, you sag again, until your lungs suck for air. You push your weight on your ankles, until your screaming nerves force you to sag again. You alternate between these two agonies, knowing it may take hours, perhaps days, until exhaustion and dehydration finally send you into the black oblivion that is your only hope.

And the entire time you take to die, your body will only be a scant foot or two off the ground that would give you life—if only someone would take you down during the long, endless hours of horror.

This death Jesus accepted . . . for sins he did not commit.

The Sign on the Cross

> Pilate had a notice prepared and fastened to the cross. It read: JESUS OF NAZARETH, THE KING OF THE JEWS. Many of the Jews read this sign, for the place where Jesus was crucified was near the city, and the sign was written in Aramaic, Latin and Greek.
>
> JOHN 19:19–20

ONLY PILATE CAN EXPLAIN WHY HE INSTRUCTED THE sign to be worded as it was.

To be sure, it was customary for the charges against a criminal to be chalked in legible letters on a board. As the criminal bore his cross to the execution site, the board hung by a rope from the cross or was carried ahead by a herald.

Some might believe it was Pilate's intention to mock both Jesus and the troublesome Jews who had forced Pilate to declare the capital sentence. Yet Pilate had done his best to set Jesus free, and it seems more likely that if mockery was his goal, Pilate's target was simply the religious Jews so determined to kill Jesus. (If so, it must have given Pilate satisfaction to deny the chief priests their demand to have the wording changed, as told in John 19:21, 22.)

Perhaps, instead, Jesus' simple words of truth and obvious innocence during the trial had touched Pilate enough that the hardened soldier actually felt Jesus deserved this dignity in his final hours.

Either way, the inscriptions stood—in Aramaic, Latin, and Greek.

Close readers of the Gospels will note that the

inscription is worded slightly differently in each of the accounts. A reasonable explanation is that each Gospel writer chose a different inscription to translate. John, for example, gives us the Aramaic version—most Jews read this language, so it makes sense that the longest and most offensive inscription to them was written in Aramaic.

Aramaic, Latin, and Greek.

More significant than an explanation for discrepancies, however, is the witness given by the use of all three languages.

Latin was the official language of Rome.

Greek was most commonly used for communication throughout the empire.

Aramaic reached the Jews of Israel.

The inscriptions, then, covered the intellectual, social, and religious spectrum of any who read the sign.

Yes, Pilate had his own reasons for posting the sign the way he did.

But God, who has purpose in everything, ensured that even this seemingly trivial detail worked to advance the kingdom for which Jesus gave his life.

Higher

(Jesus' thoughts from the Cross)

Dark day crowning,
Screaming, chanting,
Sounding in my ear.
Pounding, driving,
Ringing, stinging,
Take my thoughts away
To a brighter place.

Higher, higher
Than the pain that I feel,
Take me
Higher, higher.
Let Your holy love reveal;
And plunge me
Deeper, deeper
Than these nails can drive me.
Take me
Higher, higher, Father.

Children laughing,
And lepers healing
In the waters of sweet
      forgiveness—
Jordon, Galilee,
The lame are walking
By the shining sea.
Oh take me . . . .

Higher, higher
Than the pain that I feel . . . .

Can You hear me,
Hear the sound of my pain?
Can You hear me?
I can hear You.

❀ CINDY MORGAN

The Penitent Criminal

> Then he said,
> "Jesus, remember
> me when you come
> into your kingdom."
>
> LUKE 23:42

LUKE RECORDS THE CONVERSATION BETWEEN THE TWO criminals on the cross without adding what a novelist today surely would—agony and fear.

For a man on the cross, impaled flesh shrieked pain. Tortured lungs fought to pull breath against the body's weight hanging fully from extended arms. The mind fought the horror of death's certain arrival.

Imagine the first criminal, then, drawing on anger and rage and fear to find the energy to hurl insults, doing anything to deflect his mind from his own fate. "Aren't you the Christ? Save yourself and us."

Listen to the second criminal gasping each word of his response, syllables punctuated with groans. "We . . . are . . . punished . . . justly . . ." He pauses, waiting for the strength to speak further, hardly able to remain coherent but determined to defend Jesus. " . . . For we are getting what we deserve . . . but this man . . . has done nothing wrong."

Then we hear the criminal's final recorded words—not a cry to a loved one, not a declaration of defiance against an uncaring world, but an urgent plea: "Jesus, remember me when you come into your kingdom."

From a Jewish viewpoint, his words are more than remarkable.

Capital punishment, as prescribed by the laws of Moses, had two purposes. The first was to "purge evil from the land" (Deut. 21:21; 22:21).

The second purpose, expounded by Rabbinical teachings, concerned not society, but the guilty individual. His death served as the expiation of his sins. When a man or woman was about to be stoned, for example, it was customary for a confession to be requested ten cubits from the execution site, and the standard formal response was "May my death be an atonement for all my sins."

It is remarkable then, that this man, a Jew in the first century A.D., would have thoughts about the possibility of forgiveness. And that he would at that moment—the point of Jesus' ultimate human helplessness and humiliation—have the faith to recognize Jesus as the true Messiah, master of a kingdom.

No one else but the Son of God could have offered a single sentence capable of speaking so much to a man in need of comfort, a man so unaware of spiritual teaching. "I tell you the truth, today you will be with me in paradise."

In that one sentence, Christ assured him—and us—of truths we can cling to in any storm:

The soul lives beyond the body.

Christ and his paradise of love await the soul.

This paradise is freely given to all who ask through Christ.

With that answered plea, the criminal's death became a voyage, not into darkness but into light. For there on the cross, in that one sentence, in that one glorious moment, Jesus threw open to all the gates to the Kingdom of Heaven.

Take My Life

(Mary Magdalene's song at the cross)

Who can say
When life is over?
The silver cord breaks,
Our breath returns to God.
Will we walk through fields of clover,
Or soar up high
Through valleys deep and wide?

I cannot know
All that's waiting there,
But until that day
This is my prayer . . .
Take my life,
Take away all the shattered dreams
        in me
And give me love that will last forever.
Take my life,
Give me the love that

Makes me free,
'Cause I believe
That your love can save
Even a wretch like me.

This race is not
Just for the runners.
Some of us walk,
While others barely crawl.
We make our way through spring
        and winter,
Leaning on strength
That strengthens all.
And when the sunlight fades
        from morning,
You'll still be burning in my eyes.

❋ CINDY MORGAN

Jesus' Pain

U NTIL A PERSON HAS BEEN IN THE DEEP, BLACK VALLEY OF anguish, it is impossible to truly understand the agony of the soul.

Yet even for those who cannot feel that agony, the evidence is easy to see. Soul pain—so deep and black and without hope—drives some to alcohol. Others to drugs. Or to the plunder of promiscuity. Self-mutilation. Even suicide.

When we think of Jesus on the cross, we often think only of the incredible physical torture his body must have borne.

Yet wouldn't his soul have been even more tortured? His infinite love rejected. On the edge of a chasm between himself and his Father. Looking down on his weeping mother and heartbroken friends—all for the sake of the people who were crucifying him.

When those whose own souls have been in the deep, black valley of unrelieved anguish look to the man on the cross for peace, they understand what others cannot— there were probably moments when Jesus welcomed the distraction of the nails pounded into his hands.

Forgive Them

*After the Passover lamb
had been killed and its blood
sacrificed, the lamb was placed
on wooden staves where priests
would expertly skin it and remove
the innards for burning at the
altar. To keep the sacrificial
lamp pure for the Passover
meal, it was extremely
important for the priests
not to break any bones
of the lamb in this process.
To Jesus' Jewish followers, then,
it was highly significant that the
soldiers did not break his legs
to hasten his death on the cross.*

ON CRUCIFIXION, A MAN HUNG ONLY A FEW FEET OFF the ground. Bored soldiers stood nearby, waiting for his death. His loved ones, perhaps, also stood nearby, weeping or offering consolation. Others might be there out of morbid curiosity, or if they were victims of the criminal, to take satisfaction in watching his punishment.

It might be a small crowd. Or a large crowd.

But surely, from his vantage point above the crowd, a man on the cross would see everyone nearby.

What did Jesus see? His eyes saw his mother, of course, whom he put in the care of John. He saw his women friends weeping. Some of the other disciples, perhaps. And certainly the religious authorities who were determined to view his death.

But his heart saw much more. His heart saw the inner pain and burdens each person bore.

A Pharisee was worried about his son, who preferred wine and harlots to religious instruction. A woman was grieving the loss of her child. A soldier was trying to deny the peculiar agony that comes with doubts about a wife's faithfulness. Each of them—as with us all—keeping fears private and guilt out of sight. Each of them—as with us all—hiding the heartache and sorrow that comes with life lived apart from God.

Jesus knew what could heal them and give them peace—God's love. Given freely.

Yet from the cross, the very cross he had accepted to bring them God's love, his heart also saw that most of the people weren't even aware they needed to be rescued. So intent on their lives apart from God's presence, they did not bother to look to God for help. They rejected God as the answer.

Just as they had rejected Jesus.

What anguish for him. To look down with love—so desperate to rescue them he was willing to give his life—and know, there from the cross, that the people hurting him would have no part of his love, no part of the one way to find relief from their misery.

And so his plea.

Forgive them, Father, for they know not what they are doing.

Forgive them, Father. They are so lost, they cannot understand they need to be found.

Forgive them, Father. Only You can bring them peace.

Forgive us, Father. We are not so different from those gathered around the cross.

A Stumbling Block

> But we preach
> Christ crucified:
> a stumbling block to
> Jews and foolishness
> to Gentiles.
>
> 1 CORINTHIANS 1:23

FOR EARLY PREACHERS LIKE PAUL, THE FOUNDATION OF the gospel was the central truth about Jesus: his death on a cross led to resurrection on the third day.

While this is the same foundation for the gospel today, in Paul's time the implications were much different.

A man crucified was a criminal.

So the Jews would have to believe that their long-promised, all-powerful Messiah was a man who accepted a tortured death of ultimate humiliation.

Gentiles of Paul's time, without the generations-long promise of a Messiah as their heritage, would have to put their faith in a man who sweat blood in fear, lost a civil trial to the Romans, and died nearly naked in front of a jeering crowd.

While the legends of the Greek and Roman gods portrayed beauty and nobility, for proud men in the intensely patriarchal societies of that time, there was nothing heroic or manly about Jesus or his disciples in the last days before the crucifixion.

Judas betrayed. Peter denied. Jesus asked that the cup be removed. The other disciples fled. A stranger had to carry the cross. Death arrived with no dramatic rescue to intervene.

The accounts of those final days show the brutal honesty of the Gospel writers. There is no public-relations spin put on the events, no euphemisms to cast the truth in a kinder light.

Instead, the writers show themselves in full light. They write openly of their misunderstandings of Jesus and his kingdom teachings. They describe their doubts, shame, cowardice, and failings. They never flinch from telling it the way it was.

No wonder then . . . *a stumbling block to the Jews and foolishness to the Gentiles.*

And to us?

The Cocoon

> Joseph took the body,
> wrapped it in a clean
> linen cloth, and placed
> it in his own new
> tomb that he had cut
> out of the rock.
>
> MATTHEW 27:59

*I*N JERUSALEM THERE IS DISAGREEMENT OVER THE LOCATION of the tomb.

The traditional site is the Church of the Holy Sepulcher, visited yearly by tens of thousands who walk with silent awe past the place where it is said the three crosses once stood.

History tells us it was there, in 326 A.D., that Queen Helena, mother to the Christian emperor Constantine, on a mission to establish holy sites, decided Christ had been crucified and buried. The original church, built by Constantine, was destroyed by the Persians three centuries later, rebuilt, then destroyed again by an earthquake one hundred years later in 746 A.D. The church standing there today, built in the twelfth century by the Crusaders, is one of the oldest standing buildings in Jerusalem.

Other people, arguing in archeological terms, say the correct location of the tomb is the site known as the Garden Tomb just outside the walls of the Old City. It is located in an area that appears to have been an olive garden. It could have belonged to a wealthy man like Joseph of Arimathea.

Near this garden is a hill that looks eerily like a skull. *Golgotha.* It was not named, as many think, for skulls abandoned around the execution sites; Jewish law forbids exposure of human bones. Instead, as anyone can see even today, the hill is a high, rounded, rocky plateau shaped like the dome of a man's head, worn away by wind and rain to a dull gray. Two shallow caves side-by-side, and a lower, larger cave centered below, form the two eyes and gaping mouth of a skull. At certain times of the day, when the sunlight casts black shadows across those depressions, such is the vision of a gaunt face that you can almost hear an ancient wind moan across its barren stone, echoing the cries and groans and cursings of all the men who ever died tortured deaths within sight of those dead, dark eyes.

The tomb, too, speaks of the divine body that was gently laid there by Joseph of Arimathea. Where Jesus' body would have rested, one end of the tomb is hollowed out an extra few inches—as if workers had first designed it for the owner of the tomb, then changed it at the last minute to accommodate a taller body.

What really matters, of course, is that the tomb was empty when the women arrived.

And empty later when Peter and John arrived.

After all, what is more important? The cocoon? Or the butterfly, free and far from the empty wrapping?

Alive and Well

Who did you call Him,
When the people ran to His strong
   healing hands?
Do you know?
Who did you call Him,
When the children danced in the
   warmth of His glance?
Do you know?
You raised your voices in doubt.
His blood is falling on you.
   Do you know?

Shattered darkness brought the light,
Poured the blood and pierced
   the night.
Sweet salvation shine the light,
My Savior, He's alive and well.
Shattered darkness brought the light,
Poured the blood and pierced
   the night.
Sweet salvation shine the light,
My Savior, He's alive and well.
Who did you call Him?

When He raised the dead, all of
   Hell's demons fled.
Do you know?
Who did you call Him?
Did He demand your all and
   in your pride
Now you fall once again?

I've touched the wounds in His side,
And He dried the tears in my eyes,
And He's alive—
My Savior, He's alive.
Hallelujah . . . He's alive
Hallelujah.

Do you believe it? He's alive,
   He's alive and well!
Shattered darkness brought the light,
Poured the blood and pierced
   the night.
Oh won't you lift your voice and sing,
Yeah, sweet salvation.

✤ CINDY MORGAN

The Carpenter's Cloth

> Then Simon Peter, who was behind him, arrived and went into the tomb. He saw the strips of linen lying there, as well as the burial cloth that had been around Jesus' head. The cloth was folded up by itself, separate from the linen.
>
> JOHN 20:6, 7

*D*URING JESUS' TIME THERE WAS ONE WAY A CARPENTER LET THE contractor know a job was finished. A signature, so to speak.

Imagine a hot afternoon in Galilee. Jesus has completed the final pieces of a job he has worked on for several days. The hair of his strong forearms is matted with sawdust and sweat. His face is shiny with heat. He takes a final—and welcome—drink of cool water from a leather bag.

Then, standing to the side of his work, he pours water over his face and chest, splashing it over his arms to clean himself before his journey home. With a nearby towel, he pats his face and arms dry.

Finally, Jesus folds the towel neatly in half, and then folds it in half again. He sets it on the finished work and walks away. Later, whoever arrives to inspect the work will see the towel and understand its simple message. The work is finished.

Christ's disciples, of course, knew this carpenter's tradition. On a Sunday of sorrow, three years after Jesus had set aside his carpenter tools, Peter will crouch to look into an empty tomb and see only the linens that the risen Lord has left behind.

A smile will cross Peter's face as his sorrow is replaced by hope, for he will see the wrap that had covered Jesus' face. It has been folded in half, then folded in half again and left neatly on the floor of the tomb.

Peter understands. The carpenter has left behind a simple message.

It is finished.

Praise the King

Praise Him in the morning
For tall and lofty trees,
And praise Him in the evening
For children on their knees,
Oh and praise Him in the noon day
For gentle birds that sing,
Oh praise Him all ye people,
Praise the King,
And praise Him for a peaceful
porch
And rocking chairs that sway,
Praise Him for the rolling hills
Where children laugh and play,
Oh and praise Him for the
wandering souls
That never lost their way,
Oh praise Him all ye people,
Praise the King,

Praise the King . . .
Let it ring . . .
Praise the king,
And praise Him for the blood
that fell
And bloomed a rose that day,
And praise Him that he suffered
through the guilt, the grief,
the shame,
Oh and praise Him that his tender
love will still forgive today,
Oh praise Him all ye people,
praise the King,

❀ CINDY MORGAN

LIST OF ILLUSTRATIONS